D1615392

WIPED
OUT?

WIPED
OUT?

THE JEROME WILSON STORY

WIPED OUT?

THE JEROME WILSON STORY
BY MARK TURLEY & JEROME WILSON

First published by Pitch Publishing, 2015

Pitch Publishing
A2 Yeoman Gate
Yeoman Way
Durrington
BN13 3QZ
www.pitchpublishing.co.uk

© Jerome Wilson with Mark Turley, 2015

ISBN 978-1-90962-058-4

Typesetting and origination by Pitch Publishing

Printed by Melita Press, Poala, Malta

Contents

Special Acknowledgements

AS a boxer you have to make many sacrifices hoping that all will work out well in the end. Sometimes the gamble pays off but on this occasion my boxing career never did turn out how I hoped.

A lot of parts of my life took second place to boxing. I spent a great deal of time away from friends and family due to work obligations and training regimes. This took a massive toll on my relationships and put pressure on me to try and justify all the time spent away. I put up with a lot of crap and kept trying, so that one day I'd be able to give my partner, kids, myself and family a better life. Much of the time I was living away from them, in a different city (Sheffield), doing what I needed to do throughout the week then whizzing back up to Bradford for the weekend.

I really do have a good woman. Michelle has stuck with me through some of the hardest of times, I've put her through so much and she still stays by my side. So I dedicate massive love and respect to her. And I want to take this opportunity to publicly say sorry for all the selfish things I have done in the eight years we have been together.

My Mum, Brinneth, has always been there for me too. No mother should have to see their child in the condition I was in, so I also dedicate this book to her. She always worried about me entering the boxing arena and didn't want me to be a boxer. Despite that she attended the majority of my fights to show support for what I was trying to do. The aftermath of my final contest has caused so much pain, division, hurt and shock for us all. She has had to endure all of that. Sorry Mum.

My coach Ian Baines helped me learn to believe in myself, love boxing again, and to enjoy it as I had at the start. He always said everything as it was, straight down the line. He didn't make any promises he couldn't keep. He got me fit, offered me support and taught me so many new things. He didn't even ask for money. 'What's ten per cent of nothing?' He would say. He did it because he loved it. For this I have massive respect for him.

My brother Marvin is the one person who has been there at every single pro fight I have had. He always supported me 100 per cent, and travelled with me to so many different places. I always knew I could depend on him, no matter what.

I would also like to thank Mark Turley and Pitch Publishing for giving me the opportunity to get my story out there. I have trusted Mark with many of my deep and most personal thoughts, opinions and life experiences. He has managed to unlock some

Special Acknowledgements

memories I thought were long gone but were just festering in the back of my mind. Thank you Mark, and may you continue to write thought-provoking and interesting books for all to read and enjoy.

Jerome Wilson, June 2015

Foreword by Curtis Woodhouse

Professional footballer 1997 to 2005, representing Sheffield United, Birmingham City, Hull City and England Under-21. Turned to boxing in 2005, ultimately becoming British light-welterweight champion in 2014. Former stablemate and training partner of Jerome Wilson.

JEROME was the most talented athlete I came across in 20 years of professional sport. He was very, very gifted. I believe if Jerome chose any sport he would have excelled at it.

His boxing career took a different path to mine. We shared probably over a thousand rounds of sparring together and whenever I had a big fight Jerome was always my first port of call. When it came to getting my preparation sorted, when I needed tough rounds, it would be Jerome who I would approach to spar. I did not enjoy our sparring sessions one little bit and came off second best almost every time, but I knew no matter who I was fighting they wouldn't have Jerome's speed. When I did well in our spars it let me know I was ready for fight night.

Boxing isn't always about who's the best, it's a business. If you sell loads of tickets, make big money for your promoters and you can fight a little bit you will be a champion of some sort. Jerome could fight a lot but was never a ticket seller. He was somewhat unknown by the mainstream, but anybody who sparred him will tell you he was one of the best kept secrets in British boxing. I've witnessed with my own eyes Jerome taking champions to school in sparring, bamboozling British, European and world title holders. He was that good in the gym. If you ask anybody who trained alongside him, they will tell you the same.

Sometimes the dream of being a boxer and the reality of it are two separate things and having to work full-time and raise a family alongside trying to prepare for a fight are close to impossible. I was very fortunate. I came on the back of playing professional football and sold lots of tickets because of this. I won the British title but had only ten per cent of Jerome's talent. Selling tickets and being a 'name' gave me opportunities Jerome never got.

The night Jerome got injured I had been sparring with him the weeks leading up to his fight. He was his usual slick self. I was commentating on the fight and knew instantly when he went down that he was badly hurt. I was heartbroken when he left the ring on a stretcher. I went to the hospital afterwards. It was touch and go if he would make it through the night. I really couldn't believe it. How could this be? I knew people had been injured and even died in boxing before but never anybody I worked so closely with and was a friend.

Fortunately Jerome pulled through, showing the grit and determination he had when we sparred. Jerome's injury really affected me. It made me realise that this could happen to any of us. I would only fight once more after the injury happened. I toyed with the idea of making a comeback but it had hit home to me how dangerous this sport is. I used to tell myself if it can happen to Jerome, it can happen to me.

It's great that Jerome is still with us I find his journey an inspirational one. I'll never forget his talent as a fighter and I'll never forget the night he got injured.

After his injury I did a charity boxing event to raise some money for him to help with his rehabilitation and his family. He asked me why would I do that? That took me by surprise. Whenever I needed help with my sparring Jerome would always be there to give me the rounds and the preparation I needed. The least I could do was try and help him when he needed me.

I look forward to seeing what Jerome does next. He's just one of those people that seems to do everything well. If he needs any help along the way, just like he would always do for me, I'll always be there to give a helping hand.

Curtis Woodhouse, April 2015

Introduction

BROKEN bits of information travelled down from the north – British champ Curtis Woodhouse said he was the best he'd trained with. Three time world title challenger Ryan Rhodes called him 'Sheffield's Mayweather'. Highly-respected manager and promoter Dave Coldwell repeatedly said he had world-class speed.

In any field of sports writing I've always felt the most interesting stories come from the experiences of two kinds of athlete. The first are undiscovered or unappreciated talents, blossoms yet to bloom. The second are those who defy stereotype. Jerome Wilson was both.

As a writer, hearing and sharing his story feels how I imagine it is to be a botanist who has discovered a new species of butterfly or a DJ that stumbles across a rare, sought-after piece of vinyl in a huge warehouse. He is an uncommon find among the sweat and snot of the fight game, an introvert – quiet, reflective but physically exceptional. A defensive virtuoso with KO power. Whispers whirred down the wires.

'He's so quick, so sharp, no one can touch him in sparring. He just needs to get his mind right and the world's at his feet. He could go right to the top.'

Fame and glory are fickle things. They were not Jerome's destiny. His path led him elsewhere.

It's the stuff cult heroes are made of.

* * * * *

I'd never met anyone with such a terrible injury before. It was like a movie special-effect. His head literally had a slice cleaved out of it.

'I'm feeling a bit nervous,' he said.

'Don't worry.' I switched on my dictaphone 'It'll be fine.'

It was February 2015 and we were sitting upstairs in a house near Bradford. My host was a short, compact, Afro-Caribbean guy who moved around symmetrically on the balls of his feet. Balletic, despite the conspicuous defect up top. On first impression he seemed in pretty good spirits.

As we had introduced ourselves I found it difficult not to stare at the area where surgeons had removed a bone flap – a quarter of his skull, from above and behind his right ear, leaving a mango-sized indentation. The skin there sagged down like a parachute caught between two trees. An angry scar circled the crater.

While he made affable small-talk, making light of his situation, you could actually see his brain undulate below the skin. It was unsettling and fascinating at the same time.

Is that what our brains do when we speak?

His voice was quiet. He mumbled. Sometimes he slurred his words.

Introduction

The Greek scribe Philo once wrote, 'Be kind, for everyone you meet is fighting a great battle.' Never before had I felt so acutely in the presence of someone who was battling.

It was in every gesture. He wanted to reach out to someone.

'This will be my therapy,' he told me.

At the same time it contradicted everything he stood for to become an object of pity – he still had his fighter's pride. Here was a warrior who could no longer go to war with other men. For the rest of his days he would only fight himself.

'Shall we watch it then?' he said, hovering over the laptop.

I hesitated.

'Do you think you'll be all right?' I asked. 'Are you going to burst into tears on me or something?'

He inhaled deeply.

'I don't think so, but if I do...'

He clicked play and together we began to watch the recording of his final fight, just the two of us. It was five months on from that tragic evening and his first viewing, too. He had waited to see it with me, an ignoble honour. Although I knew how the contest ended, I wasn't sure what to expect.

Mostly he sat in silence. Here and there he sighed. Sometimes he criticised his own performance.

'Look, I wasn't sharp enough with the jab.'

'He was wide open, I should have nailed him.'

'Shouldn't have got caught with that one.'

When the awful end came and his on-screen self lay stricken, the skin under his eyes wrinkled. He traced his scar absent-mindedly with one finger. I felt he had expended a ton of emotional energy.

'It's like watching somebody else,' he whispered at last, head rippling. 'Madness.'

I needed space, suggested a break. He agreed. Outside the house I walked, breathed some Yorkshire air. Nearby I found a sunlit hill, which I scaled until the village of Shipley spread below me like a map. A faint smell of bonfires hung in the wind. A couple of kids ran past, chasing a dog.

I sat there and thought long and hard about this sport we call boxing.

There is irony in the fact that 'Wipeout' Wilson's story is only made extraordinary through great misfortune. And that irony is gruesome. In the frantic final minute of his 11th professional fight, he all-but died. Knocked out, then carried out, his survival chances were haphazard and delicate, like dust on a breeze. Somehow, he pulled through.

The life he had known for so long, the fighter's life, training, dieting, pushing his boundaries, was finished in an instant by a right hand.

His momentum moved him on to the punch, doubling the impact. In boxing speak, it 'switched his lights off'.

Immediately unconscious, Jerome toppled like a chain-sawed tree. As he made his descent, neck loose, he was caught again with a left. The back of his head bounced off the boards. There was an almost imperceptible twitch in his legs. Then stillness, complete stillness.

Cue panic.

Introduction

After frantic attempts to revive him and with his attendant family in hysterics, Jerome had to be stretchered away. He did not open his eyes to start his new life for ten days. While in that prolonged limbo, neither alive nor dead, he underwent something profound.

'Subdural haematoma' – whisper those words around fighters. They are like a voodoo curse. While most claim to accept the knowledge that death or debilitating injury can come at any time, it is not, for obvious reasons, something much discussed in gyms and training camps. Like the fight game's spectre at the window, the chance of fatal or near-fatal damage hovers with invisible menace whenever two competitors climb into a ring. Of the various forms of brain damage that can be sustained through a career of regular bouts and daily sparring, it is the most common life-threatening affliction.

Tunny Hunsacker, a former Golden Gloves winner who became a trial-horse American pro and boxed Muhammad Ali on his debut, was thus afflicted in 1962, spent nine days in a coma and was never the same again, deteriorating so rapidly in middle age that from his mid-50s he required full-time care in a nursing home. In the UK's recent history, Charlie Payton (2015), Jerome Wilson (2014), Michael Norgrove (2013), Kieran Farrell (2012) and JonJo Finnegan (2012) have all had careers cut short and lives affected by it. Going further back, Michael Watson,

Paul Ingle, Spencer Oliver and many others were similarly struck down. A complete list of names would stretch for pages.

n the worst cases, such as that of James Murray, a Scottish bantamweight knocked out by Drew Docherty in 1995, or East Londoner Bradley Stone, who challenged Richie Wenton for the British super bantamweight title in 1994, death follows shortly after. Zambia-born Londoner Norgrove survived for nine days after collapsing in the ring, before his injuries proved fatal.

In others, where surgery is more successful, mobility, vision and cognitive functions are usually drastically impaired. The most-remembered example of this is the 'G-Man', Gerald McLellan, from Illinois USA who went down blinking in the tenth round of a titanic battle with Britain's Nigel Benn in 1995, never to recover. To this day and until his last, McLellan, a lithe, mantis-like puncher at his peak, remains near deaf, wheelchair bound and blind. While boys in gyms the world over fantasise of world championship glory, sports cars and piles of money, the G-Man's destiny, perhaps in some ways worse than death, represents every fighter's unspoken nightmare.

Although most sufferers lose large parts of themselves, others have fared somewhat better. Former undisputed world middleweight champion Jermain Taylor, from Arkansas, USA, was stricken with a minor form of the injury after being knocked out in the 12th by Arthur Abraham in 2009.

On the surface he made a full recovery, although warning signs were still noted. Taylor began to exhibit mood swings and persistent short-term memory loss, often completely forgetting what had been said to him moments before.

Despite this the state of Nevada went against precedent and accepted his application for relicensing in 2011. Amid cries that he was unfit to box and would be seriously hurt, Taylor proved his doubters wrong and managed to recapture the IBF version of the world title in August 2014.

Yet alarm bells continued to ring. In the months following his title win, his behaviour became increasingly erratic. A series of bizarre incidents were reported involving firearms, violence and threatening behaviour to women and children. He was arrested late in 2014, at which point his attorney Hubert Alexander explained, 'Everyone is saying this isn't the Jermain Taylor they know. We're trying to figure out who the heck it is.' Taylor was subsequently referred to a mental hospital in January 2015 for full evaluation and assessment.

As shown by Taylor's case, any discussion of serious boxing injuries taps into deeper, universal issues. What does it mean to damage the brain? Why does it change who we are? How does the brain shape our identity and reality? These things are not fully understood.

Even now, in the 21st century medical science has more questions than answers regarding our most important organ. It remains a thing of mystery. For those who hold some kind of religious belief it is probably in that pulsating soft, pink tissue that our link to God can be found. For others, it is the core of our humanity.

There are more neurones in the human nervous system than there are stars in the galaxy. The brain sits atop all that, conducting the orchestra enigmatically. It filters our entire experience of being alive. To all extents, it is the person. When it sustains damage everything we take for granted is affected.

An SDH, as it is known in medical circles, can be either acute (sudden) or chronic (gradual) and occurs when blood vessels rupture in the space between the skull and the brain, known as the subdural cavity. More often than not this is caused by rapid rotational force through heavy impact. Although this can occur in many sports and circumstances, a meaty punch landing on the jaw at an angle, such as a well-timed hook or uppercut creates the perfect conditions for it.

The tearing of these tiny veins and capillaries causes bleeding, then clotting. This exerts internal pressure, the amount of which depends on the size of the bleed. There have been cases reported where the pressure was so great, that upon reaching the operating theatre and having an incision made to gain access, blood has fountained from the wound, travelling several feet through the air and spattering the walls.

When Jerome was struck by an SDH on 12 September 2014, I knew his name, but did not know him. Like many others I saw the media coverage and was dismayed to observe that his opponent, in a moment of wild elation at the win, knelt down and kissed his head, then jumped up, making a throat-cutting gesture at the audience. All while Jerome lay motionless.

This macabre scene, like something from an ancient coliseum, seemed so out of kilter with 21st century morality. The sight of a young man on the cusp of death, his opponent gloating and the audience in uproar made me question whether it was all worth it. How could it be?

Wilson was taken to hospital. While ambulance crewmen scrambled to keep him alive, sirens blaring, speeding across the city, back in the arena the show continued. Contestants for the next bout prepared to make entrances, cheered on by platoons of raucous supporters. Nearly flat-lining, Jerome had been whisked away – out of sight and mind.

Like everyone else connected to the sport I hoped for a speedy recovery. These sorts of incidents are reminders of the moral tightrope we tip-toe on with our involvement in boxing. Yes, there is discipline and honour among the blood, the sport can save young men from the streets, but the brutal reality of competing in the ring can and frequently does ruin lives. We have to be honest about that, don't we?

Initial signs did not look good. Upon reaching hospital Jerome had a seizure, like an epileptic fit. They operated, did all they could, but if the pressure continued to build in the wrong direction he would die. He was placed on a ventilator in a medically induced coma. His family, including long-term girlfriend Michelle and three-year-old daughter Serenity, both of whom had been at ringside were told to prepare for the worst. Doctors thought it unlikely he would last the night.

Various crises were averted over the following 72 hours. A week and a half later he defied predictions and began to regain consciousness. Showing great compassion and camaraderie, Wilson's boxing 'family' rallied round and his former training partners Ryan Rhodes and Curtis Woodhouse organised a fundraiser at which Woodhouse boxed an exhibition with Hull's Tommy Coyle. TV and newspapers carried the story.

On Halloween, he was discharged. His recovery was something of a miracle, it was said. He was talking and walking and more-or-less fully functioning. Pictures appeared of him smiling and giving thumbs-up at cameras.

On the same day I received a message from a Sheffield-based ex-fighter called Daniel Thorpe. Daniel had trained with Jerome for many years and said he was going to visit him. I sent a copy of my last book, *Journeymen*, in the post for Thorpey to give him as a present.

After that I continued to follow reports of Jerome's progress. By early January he had reconnected with the world and was noting thoughts and feelings down as a diary. Clearly he was having quite a tough time and struggling with his new reality. He floated the prospect of doing a book and asked for help on the internet. Following the usual series of comments, shares and retweets, his request ended up in my inbox.

I listened to Jerome speak and read some things he had written. Everything he once had been had gone. He was lost. He questioned his own sanity. I had a feeling this was something I should do. You are holding the result.

It is not and never will be my aim to attack boxing. I have been connected to it in one way or another all my life and always will be, even if just as a spectator.

Introduction

For various reasons, boxing is a part of me that I cannot let go.

But I also strongly believe that we should be able to discuss its dangers with openness. Most importantly, young people entering the sport should be made aware of the risks they are taking. No one should walk towards the sound of the guns blindfolded.

Jerome's personal reactions to massive brain trauma can make for challenging reading, but through the process of jotting them down he was able to regain some sense of self. Be clear on one thing before you start – opening up his experiences and innermost thoughts to the public, during such a difficult and doubt-ridden period of his life shows great courage.

Jerome is not stupid. There are no guarantees with SDH and he knows he faces an uncertain future. It was my privilege to help him take his first steps into it by collaborating with him to write this book. I hope it helps him begin his post-boxing journey and serves as a reminder to all readers that the sport has two sides.

Wipeout Wilson loved boxing. It was everything to him. But now he knows better than most that after that last bell has rung, the world can be a dark and inhospitable place.

Mark Turley, May 2015

'As you know Calvin I'm in a very dangerous fight tomorrow night. If anything was to happen to me, promise me that you will do your best to help out with the house, your mum and the kids. I do love you like you were my own child, I may be hard on you at times, it is because I want you to do well in life and not be a lazy bum, not that I'm picking on you, I just see you can do more. Cool?

'Life is not always easy; you must make sacrifices and do what you can to support yourself and your family. So shout loud for me and I will see you after the fight.'

Message written by Jerome Wilson to his stepson Calvin, 11 September 2014

Part One – Old Life

'All that we see, or seem,
is but a dream within a dream.'

Edgar Allan Poe

12 September 2014, Ice Sheffield

I SAW him the night before the weigh-in. I'd finished in the gym a little while before. Just a light session to keep me loose, winding down. You don't want to expend too much energy so close to a fight. But there he was, pounding the pavement on Sheffield Road, sauna suit on, hood up. He was really going for it. I got a little knot in my stomach. It gave me a lift.

'I don't believe what I'm seeing!' I shouted, pointing through the windscreen. 'He must be crashing the weight!' He'd had those kind of problems in the past. Marvin and I shared a laugh.

But when I saw him on the scales at the Grosvenor Casino he didn't look drained. He looked big. He looked mean. He's a heavy framed guy, like his skeleton is constructed with steel girders. He's got a huge head. When we went face to face for the customary stare-down, his eyes were sunk into his skull like some sort of monster. His cheekbones looked like they'd been laid with angle-beads.

He's such an ugly bastard! We'd all laughed about it. Mum joked that he couldn't have been born from a human woman. He must have been created in some kind of experiment. We had a chuckle about that, but Mum didn't have to fight him. She didn't want me to either.

She begged me not to go through with it, over and over. She kept going on. I got fed up of hearing it. We argued. In the end I walked away and told her to shut up. Other people's negativity can get to you, can stick in your head and eat away at your confidence. I didn't need that. Not for any fight. And definitely not for this one.

We both made weight. He made it comfortably in the end, a pound lighter than me. God knows how he managed that. I wondered if the scales were broken, but that was it, it was on. There was no talking, there didn't need to be. But that couldn't hide a genuine spark of hatred, lit by what had happened between us.

To strike hard and strike true, Bruce Lee said fighters should never be angry, but should have 'emotional content'. We definitely had that, me and him.

Among the masses in attendance were three old ladies, I don't know what they were doing at a boxing weigh-in. I guess they were playing the one-arm bandits and wandered over out of curiosity. They came up to me when I was getting dressed.

'You're too cute to be a boxer,' the first said, admiring the crucifix I had on a silver chain around my neck. 'You shouldn't be fighting love, you seem far too nice,' offered the second. The third gazed at me curiously.

'I'm sure there are big things in your future,' she smiled.

I thanked them and we had a little chat.

Once the weigh-in was over and I got away from the crowds, mentally I began to slip into fight mode. It was always the same. In those long hours of slow torture before first bell I always knew what I was going to do.

They were such charged moments, so emotional. I only feared losing. I didn't fear fighting. I enjoyed it. I got butterflies and nervous tension, but no fear. I wouldn't call it fear. Definitely not fear.

It was the biggest night of my career. I knew that. Everyone around me knew it too. I'd had a make-or-break fight before, against the 'Isle of Wight Assassin', Jay Morris, in 2011. There'd been a lot riding on that one and I'd blown it. My head hadn't been right. I hadn't trained well. This was my second chance, a massive local grudge match. I had to make it count. Two Sheffield boxers with everything on the line. There had even been whispers of a contract to fight on Channel 5 if things went well. That was big stuff for a kid off a council estate like me. You rarely get second chances in boxing.

I sold most of my allotted tickets, which made a nice change. Everyone wanted to see this one. I dropped the last of them off that night. It was pleasing to know I'd done my bit. Eddie Hearn was going to be there, the country's top promoter.

I chilled out at home, had some food and an early night, slept well and awoke buzzing. The next day I sat in the garden, talking to myself, turning things over, an old habit. I read about it in a book. Self-realisation, they call it.

'You *are* good enough. You *can* do this,' I murmured, eyes shut. 'If you want to be a champion you have to show it. Think like a champion. Move like a champion. Don't be tense, stay relaxed. Now this is what you're going to do – box him, use your feet, side to side. Open the door before you walk through it. After this one you'll be looked after, get the right fights. Everything will change. It will all come from here.'

When I arrived at the venue, my manager Dave Coldwell wasn't there yet, but I saw his business partner, Spencer Fearn. I went up to the office and handed over the money from tickets with the few spares I had left. Spencer seemed pleased.

'You've done all right,' he said. He gave me some words of encouragement. I nodded and walked down to the dressing room.

My entrance music CD was in my kitbag – 'Fix Up, Look Sharp' by Dizzee Rascal. I grabbed it then spent ten minutes walking around trying to find the DJ. I caught up with him outside one of the venue bars. We spoke briefly. I made sure he understood how to cue it up. He was all smiles and back-slaps. Business time approached.

I was about to get changed when my girlfriend, Michelle arrived. We've been together eight years. She's my rock. She seemed tense though, like Mum. She wasn't happy about this one.

She's into psychics, clairvoyants and all that stuff. She believes funny things about the mind. She had a dream that I got injured, that I ended up in hospital in a coma. You don't need to hear that sort of stuff before you get in the ring.

Michelle had our three-year-old daughter Serenity with her. It was Serenity's first fight night. I'd wanted her there. I wanted her to see Daddy do well, to share my moment. I picked her up and walked around, talking to her, making her feel at home. She didn't have a clue what was happening. My 16-year-old stepson Calvin was by Michelle's side too. He's a good kid, that one.

Nobody else knew but Michelle was two and a half months pregnant. It was our little secret. I put my hand on her belly and gave her a kiss. They all wished me luck and I left, back to my changing room, back to my zone. I had to get ready for take-off. A family is like a base. They gave me a platform to launch myself from.

Soon I was tuning up, throwing shots at the pads, really letting them go. My trainer Ian was in pain, I was hitting so hard.

'What are you doing?' he said. 'Save it for the fight! You need to make sure you hit him like that. Make him even uglier!' We kept at it until my forehead moistened with sweat the muscles in my upper back spread and loosened.

'You're ready,' he said.

I nodded slowly, walked away, speaking to myself again, geeing myself up.

'Come on, you've got this, he's not quick enough, his feet aren't good enough, you can school him, in and out, keep moving, the fists can't hit what the eyes can't see.'

It was nearly time. I sat in a chair in the corner, legs stretched, eyes shut, headphones on.

Waiting.

2

Ryan, Why You?

LIKE all the best stories mine begins with a fight, a
woman, and a flash car. You might think the fight
I'm talking about would come at the end. But
my story isn't going to work like that. In this book,
the end becomes the beginning. The rest falls in place
around it. For a while it may seem haphazard, but life
often is. It's the way I've come to figure it all out.

The passage of days, weeks and years doesn't
seem that important to me anymore. Time is just an
invention, like a clock. It's something we created to
help us understand ourselves. One day you're born,
another day you die – time is a just tool to measure
and count the bit in the middle.

What you probably know already is that something
terrible happened while I was doing something I
love; fighting. People find it hard to understand how
anyone can love giving and receiving pain, but I did.
I loved fighting.

When I let my fists go I felt like I could punch
through inadequacy, smash routine, make the days

full, make them come alive. I loved learning new things. I loved the challenge. I loved the sounds of the gym, wrapped fists hitting pads, feet on boards. I loved the pungent smells of sweat and blood. I loved the little rituals, having your hands wrapped, shadow boxing. Those rituals become habits. Habits become character. Character becomes destiny. At the end of it all, I loved combat.

The truth is I didn't always. I was shy as a youngster and the only black kid in my primary school class. The others all thought I was hard just because I was black. I didn't need to fight.

If someone got cheeky, all I had to do was give them a look and they'd leave me alone. In fact, in my whole time as a kid I only got in one scrap. Imagine that? A fighter who virtually never fought!

I found school tough, English and Maths weren't my things and I was shy around girls. I know that doesn't sound much like your typical rowdy boxer, but there it is. Later on I wanted to do something to give myself more confidence, to make me believe in myself. Boxing became that thing. It gave me purpose and an identity. It became who I am.

Who I was.

Yes, I was a professional fighter. A pretty good one too, I only had 11 pro fights, winning eight, but I think I could have gone all the way. I know all fighters say that but I mean it. There's a lot more to recognising ability than looking at numbers on a record.

I had regular spars with Kell Brook. He was a weight division above me but we gave each other hell, to and fro. A month before my last fight Kell got on a plane, flew over to the States and took the world title off an American in his own backyard. That's not easy.

I matched Kell. I know I did. Some people said I was better in the gym than the ring and that might even be true, but I knew from daily experience that I could compete with someone like that – someone world-class.

One time I went to spar former world light welterweight champ Junior Witter at the famous Wincobank gym. Legendary coach Brendan Ingle pulled me to one side afterwards.

'You'll win a world title one day,' he said.

Brendan knows what he's on about, too. His fighters have won a few, but I guess that's all just words now.

The thought of injury was always in the back of mind – a possibility. I didn't ever believe it would happen to me, though. I could look after myself in there. I was fast enough, wise enough and tricky enough to avoid any dangerous situations. In our own heads, we all are.

Boxing is a psychological struggle. Fans only see the external fight, the fists landing on bodies and faces, but there's a fight going on inside each man.

Can you be your own master, swallow your fear? Not everyone can. Training drills are one thing, but how well do you cope with confrontation? When your eye swells up and you taste blood in your mouth, can you hold your nerve? I was elusive, quick. I could put my shots together.

My life-changing fight took place in Sheffield, my hometown. I don't remember much about it. I was knocked out in the sixth, I later learned, because I got careless with a naturally bigger and stronger opponent. Grudge matches can get you like that. You're too emotionally involved and before you know it you're eating shots you'd normally see before they're thrown.

Many times doctors told me how lucky I am, they didn't think I'd pull through. My unconsciousness became a prison. For a week and a half I was locked inside myself.

Getting so badly injured in a fight would be a tragedy for any boxer, but when that injury comes at the hands of one of your close friends, it's tough to come to terms with. Myself and Ryan Rhodes shared a manager in Dave Coldwell and spent many years as training partners. Life can deal you some cruel cards. How strange – that he should be the one to do this to me.

I remember the beginning of our bout at Ice Sheffield. It's a skating rink usually, which seemed appropriate. Ryan's eyes were cold and blue, like an arctic pond. There was no friendship there. I really felt his hate. He needed to cause me pain, to vent his rage. As fighters we store up our feelings then let them go in the ring – controlled fury. I could see that in him, bursting to get out. He wanted it so badly. I guess he got it.

I couldn't admit it to myself but it bothered me. A fight was about to start and I needed to feel right, but in my heart I didn't want to fight him, no matter what had passed between us.

Ryan had been British and European champion at light middleweight and fought three times for world titles. Known in his early days as the 'Spice Boy', he grew up training in the famous Ingle gym, with legends like Naseem Hamed and Johnny Nelson. They had similar styles the three of them, hands down, fluid footwork, switch-hitting. Ryan will always be associated with that era of Sheffield boxing. In Yorkshire he's like a member of a fighting royal family.

My memories of the fight itself are few. I had a plan in my mind – move a lot, don't stand and trade, he's bigger, he's boxed at a high level but he's old, so keep him off guard, be smarter, use speed. The crowd were so loud. It was frenetic. Just before the end we clinched. As the ref broke us I realised I was glad of the breather, it was such a difficult contest.

And then everything was white.

Just white, everywhere.

And a sound like wind, rushing in my ears.

I went away for a while. Then the white began to smudge. It became thicker and heavier in places, thinner, almost transparent in others. It formed white walls, white ceiling, white sheets. I was lying on a bed and my Dad was holding my hand.

'I love you son,' he was saying. 'I love you. Talk to me. Say something.'

I thought I was in Heaven.

The Coldwell Camp

I FIRST met Ryan when I was 19. I still remember the day. I was training at Dave Coldwell's old Hyde Park gym, in the ring with all my gear on, getting ready to spar. By that time I was a regular face down there. I'd been training with Dave for three years.

I only took up boxing by accident, if I'm honest. It wasn't something I'd been interested in as a kid. I wasn't a scrapper. I'd always been a natural athlete and gymnast. I could run fast, tumble and do back-flips from a young age. At school I loved basketball. I played for a team called Sheffield Arrows. I've never been tall but I had quick feet and a good leap. I excelled at badminton too.

When I was 16 some friends of mine, a few bad lads, started going to the boxing club. They thought it was cool. That's one of the funny things with boxing. It has a way of reaching out to the unreachables. If I'd tried to get those guys to come to the sports centre for a game of badminton they would have laughed and told me to get lost. But boxing? Rough kids all like to think they can fight. They really got into it. In the end I went along with them.

It's never easy to explain why you fall in love with something, but me and boxing just had chemistry. It was meant to be. My athleticism gave me a head start. I was easily the best of the group I went in with and the coaches all said I could do something. Everyone likes being praised. Everyone likes hearing they're talented.

I didn't like being hit, though. Getting hurt wasn't on my agenda. I was never one of these psychos who say they enjoy pain, who thrive on taking licks. I felt I could develop a style in which I would avoid my opponent's punches.

Dave lent me some videos and I watched them at home. Sugar Ray Leonard, Pernell Whittaker, Floyd Mayweather Jr – I loved the way they boxed, so clever, so mobile. I'd gawp at them for hours. I wanted to be like them. I became a boxing fan.

Although I loved training and learning, I still didn't know all the big UK names, so I wasn't familiar with Ryan. I started to spar, then between rounds I looked over. Dave was talking to this huge, fat guy.

They were laughing and chatting as if they knew each other well. The chubby chap was very thick around the middle and heavy in the legs. He had a big, baggy t-shirt on. 'Who the hell is that?' I thought. 'Is he a boxer?'

He certainly didn't look like one! He looked like he'd just rolled out of the pub. I later understood that Ryan had taken a year off after losing on a third round stoppage to Lee Blundell at the York Hall in London. Blundell was a domestic-level, southpaw beanpole from Wigan. Losing to him had put Ryan's career in meltdown.

Everyone expected Rhodes to follow his childhood mate Naseem Hamed to world honours, but it just wasn't happening for him. There are no sure-things in boxing. He'd lost his first title shot, to the Canadian Otis Grant in 1997, then Jason Matthews had hammered him for the WBO middleweight belt in Doncaster in 1999. He'd struggled a bit since then, left the Ingles, who he'd been with since his school days and been in a state of semi-retirement.

Ryan was mates with Dave from years before. They'd been stablemates back when Dave was still a fighter. Dave was in his early days as a trainer and didn't really have any big name fighters in his stable, so he was very keen to bring in Rhodes. He was still a massive name, especially in South Yorkshire and would sell bundles of tickets.

I got talking to a few people around the gym. They were all hyped about the new guy. That passed itself on to me. I watched him keenly from the first time he trained and was so impressed by his footwork. He had real quality. Even though he was fat, he could really move still!

Myself and Ryan hit it off from the beginning. We always got on. I looked up to him. I really did. I wanted to show my very best stuff when he was around and impress him. I don't know if he ever knew that, but he had that effect on me. I would raise my level because of who he was and what he'd achieved.

Once he settled in and become a fixture at the gym, he got himself back in shape quickly. We had frequent spars. I never had an easy time with him. It was very competitive and I always had to be alert. Ryan boxed at light-middle and middleweight whereas I was really a light-welter, so there was usually a stone or so (six or seven kilos) between us.

I think at the start he held himself back. I was only young and lighter than him, while he'd been world ranked. He didn't want to give me a hard time. Later on he started to view me as someone who could give him some competition. We had tough, tough spars. I really gave him a run for his money.

I learnt to be an adaptable fighter, read my opponent and make adjustments. I was good at anticipating the other guy's moves. We sparred so often I got comfortable with his style.

In all those years he only got to me once. I was 26 and already fighting professionally. He put me down with a straight right. I was finding things too easy and got careless. Dancing around, darting in and out. I left myself open. Ryan was big and heavy-handed compared to me but I jumped straight back up and finished the spar. I didn't want him to think I was hurt.

Although we were friends there were still occasional moments of tension. There often is between training partners. A hard spar can leave a bit of needle in the air. To have someone bruising your face and cracking your ribs for ten minutes, then be best mates afterwards is not always a straightforward transition.

I remember a few times Dave would have us all doing fitness tests. Everyone wanted to be top dog.

Dave would penalise us with extra exercises if we didn't beat our personal bests from before. He kept scores logged on his smartphone.

On many occasions I won. Ryan and one or two other lads didn't like it. There'd be a few looks and behind-the-back comments. I never read too much into it though. Fighters are all competitive. It's the nature of the beast.

Another time Ryan was training for a fight in London and we sparred. We were moving around, letting the shots go. The distance closed and I caught him heavily in the eye. I didn't mean to. It was just one of those things, but an injury could jeopardise his fight. That was the first time I saw him switch. He suddenly glared at me with bad intentions.

He mumbled something under his breath, face screwed, squaring up. He looked like he wanted to rip my head off.

'Oh shit!' I thought. 'What have I done here?' I wasn't sure what would happen. Dave was at ringside. He checked Ryan's eye and left us to it. Ryan calmed down a bit later.

But generally we all got along well. They were good times, the early days. There were fighters of all levels in that gym, guys like Carl Baker, Daniel Thorpe and Richie Wenton. I became the unofficial camp DJ. I'd put CDs together with reggae, dancehall, garage, a mixture of good, pumping tunes to train to. I like the rhythm and beat when I'm sweating. At the end of a session I'd have a shower, go back to the stereo and my disc would be missing. Ryan always used to nick my CDs! Always, the cheeky git. There'd be a bit of banter, he'd deny it, then I'd hear him playing my music in his car.

I decided to start a little business and make spare copies of my stuff so I could sell them for a few quid. He still bloody nicked them!

The fact is for a long time Rhodes was kind of an idol of mine, which sounds funny because you don't normally see your idols every day, but he was someone for me to look up to. He won the British title when he was only 20. And there I was, a novice only 19, or 20 years old myself, training with him, learning from him.

He had massive support. You know if you've got Ryan Rhodes on your show you're not going to have any problems with gate receipts. He'd always been a good ticket seller, but with his career and all the sponsorships and media attention he got, he was right up there. Even though he hadn't quite won a world title, he was a massive draw.

My problem was although I had ability, I found that side difficult. I didn't sell enough tickets to be well looked after, pick and choose my fights and have a career steered towards titles. There were many occasions that I missed out on opportunities and when I asked Dave why, he would say, 'Sorry mate, they only want ticket sellers for that one.'

People think boxing is a sport, all about throwing and avoiding punches. It's not though. It's a business and at the bottom end, as a novice, that means selling tickets more than anything else.

As the home fighter you will get sent a bundle of them a couple of months before the show. You have to personally punt them out to anyone you can. When you put word out, on social media and the grapevine, everyone says they'll come.

'Oh yeah, of course Jerome. One hundred per cent I'll be there. I'll take five off you mate. I'll bring my cousins and my Aunty Mary.' Then when it's time to collect the money, it's a different story.

'Sorry pal, the gas bill was high this month, I had to have some dental work done, we had to get the dog spayed. I'd love to be there but I just can't. Sorry buddy. Good luck though, yeah? I'll be with you in spirit.'

For my pro debut in 2010 about 250 people said they'd buy tickets. Do you know how many I eventually sold? 50.

Friends, family, ex-colleagues, old faces from school. You're chasing them all, almost pleading with them. It's desperate. I hated it.

If you can't sell enough it's a major black mark against your name. Normally they expect you to shift 80–100. For one of my fights, against a guy called Sid Razak in Rotherham, I only sold 15. Dave was not happy at all. It was his show and I got called into the office.

'I'm losing money by putting you on,' he told me, face stern. 'You're actually costing me money. We can't keep going like this.' I was under pressure. My future was in question. That's how it was for me. It meant I couldn't take time to build a record. I had to take chances.

A few years after Ryan joined the gym I finished my amateur career, took a break from boxing and got a job as a fitness instructor on a cruise ship. I travelled all over the world, Singapore, New Zealand, the Caribbean.

When I returned a year later, with the idea of going pro, Kell Brook, who was already one of the country's leading welterweights, had joined, as had former Premier League footballer Curtis Woodhouse. Curtis was a known face in the city through playing four seasons for Sheffield United. He sold tons of tickets, no bother. Before long Kell won the British title and became a massive name too. They joined Ryan as the camp's top boys.

It can be a dark place at times, the boxing business. Dave was my manager but those three were his priorities. The rest of us fought in their shadows, trying but not succeeding to get into the light.

The Pretty Girl

THOSE hopeful days of youth were long gone by late summer 2014 when I fought Ryan. My career had been through several phases and although Dave was still my manager he no longer trained me. I had eight wins and two defeats and was coming off a contentious points loss to the Cameroonian hardcase Serge Ambomo in my last fight. There'd been talk of a rematch, a possibility of fighting former world champ Junior Witter and a couple of other suggestions, but my rift with Ryan got out of hand so that contest was made instead. It wasn't a fight I'd ever wanted or dreamed could really happen.

Our problems began after I became involved with a cute brunette called Lori Nasri. She was a client of mine in my sideline working as a personal trainer. I worked with a lot of women and professional ethics meant I always kept my distance, but Lori had something a bit different. She was charismatic, just the wrong side of beautiful, petite, in her mid-to-late-20s. She had a kind of Middle Eastern mystique going on, with long, dark hair and a curvy figure. There was a certain sparkly eyed look she would give when she asked me questions. I felt a bit like she was going to tell me my fortune.

Over a period of months we became quite close. She trusted me, shared her feelings and stories of her life. She was married, but not happily so and was a successful businesswoman. I sometimes wondered if there was anything more to it, if something might happen between us. It had a little edge like that.

I've always been shy around ladies. I've never been the type to go on the pull in nightclubs and all that stuff. I wouldn't know what to say. In fact I'd never been to a nightclub at all until Dave asked me to go to one with him.

I was a late starter with girls. There was one that liked me at secondary school and I avoided her for a couple of weeks because I was too shy to talk to her. I didn't have my first proper girlfriend until I was 17 and she was a cousin of one of my training partners.

By the time Lori came along I was in a fully-committed relationship with my partner Michelle. We met online and got chatting. She was six years older than me and already had three kids. She was still married although separated from her husband. For those reasons some of my family weren't that keen, especially two of my sisters, but Michelle and I bonded so easily. After a few months messaging we met up and went out to watch a movie. It felt like it was meant to be.

I never found it weird, helping to raise children that weren't biologically mine. I try to be the best role model I can, provide a bit of direction and when necessary, some discipline. Three years ago we had a daughter together and just before my last fight, she became pregnant again. I wouldn't ever cheat on her. That's not who I am.

Nonetheless there was this strange atmosphere when Lori was around. I couldn't stop seeing her because she was a client and I found her very easy to talk to. She would ask me a lot of questions about my boxing career and I spoke openly.

I explained to her how well it had started, how I won my first four with two knockouts, but that things began to disintegrate after my first loss. It had been against Jay Morris on one of Dave's shows in Rotherham in 2011. He's a journeyman now, losing most fights, but he wasn't then. He'd beaten Curtis Woodhouse the year before. On the night I was completely out of sorts. My training had been interrupted, I'd had family problems. Morris was a dirty fighter too, he kept hitting me low and using his head. The ref just let him do it.

Already I hadn't been selling enough tickets to make an impact on the boxing business. Once I had a defeat it made everything doubly difficult. I told Lori how I continued training in Dave's camp with big stars who got all the attention and opportunities. She was very interested.

'Dave wants me to box in the away corner, but those guys end up losing most of their fights. They just do it for money,' I told her.

Her eyes shone. 'You don't need to do that Jerome. I'm sure you'll get your chance one day.'

I liked her company.

After one particularly energising session working mainly on core strength, we sat down for coffee. She tied her hair up and put glasses on, which made her look like a schoolteacher. She explained her vision for a new sports-business venture which she wanted to call Enterprise Sports. We brainstormed ideas. She asked if I'd consider a partnership. It sounded an exciting opportunity.

I told her that Dave had already established something based on a similar concept. He had a lot of little irons in the fire. She nodded and arched an eyebrow.

'I know that,' she said. 'That's why I want to get this going quickly. He'll be our competition. And we can do a much better job than him.'

I didn't feel 100 per cent about going behind Dave's back that way, but our relationship hadn't been perfect. If Dave had looked out for me and supported me as I believe he should, it would have been different, but you don't give total loyalty to someone who isn't giving it to you. There'd been signs that things weren't right between Dave and me.

Lori had such easy charm. I could sense success in her. She asked me about Dave's business and how it worked. I told her my experiences.

She pursed her lips. There was a short pause. Then she smiled her little smile.

'Why don't you come with me for a drive?' she said, finally. 'I'd like you to visit a specialist fat removal centre with me. There's been some new technology developed. I think you'll be very impressed.'

I shrugged. 'Okay.'

I had no further appointments or major plans that afternoon so I had no problem following her out of the gym and jumping in her car. She had a funky little BMW Z4. The interior smelt of incense.

Streets and shops soon blurred past the windows. Seventies funk played on the stereo, all wah-wah guitars and syncopated beats, until we arrived on a back street in Sheffield city centre where she parked up near a building. I had never seen the place before. It was pretty large, on several floors, like a department store.

We climbed out of the car and I followed her in through two tall doors of tinted glass.

A plan inside the door showed the site had a range of facilities. There was a casino, a fitness suite and studio room, an indoor arena, and the fat removal/ beauty clinic. The interior of the place was lush. Someone had spent millions of pounds on it.

We walked through the lobby and rode the lift to the first floor clinic. I was appalled to see pictures of really obese people and siphoned fat on the walls. I guess they wanted to shock clients into using their services, but I found it disgusting and unsettling. Lori just sauntered in like she owned the place.

'You're going to love this, Jerome,' she said. 'A process has been developed whereby one stone of body fat can be lost in around 30 minutes.'

I laughed. Having worked in the health industry for several years and become familiar with fat-loss methods through making weight for fights, I was sceptical to say the least, but agreed to hang around.

Lori headed to a treatment room set to the side of the reception desk. She entered and nodded to a male technician dressed in white. I hovered by the door.

She stripped down to her underwear, threw her clothes over a rail and fastened her hair. She was very attractive, but had some cellulite around her thighs and backside. Behind her were two person-sized machines. It looked like something from science-fiction.

She smiled at me again as she climbed the steps into one of them. It was a sort of metal cocoon wrapped in a white, leathery material. There was a circular hole at one end for her head.

I was unnerved, if I'm telling the truth. Everything was white, clinical, professional, but also deeply strange. I had never seen anything like it. Lori was enclosed in the machine. She revolved slowly. It was hypnotic. There was a look of serenity on her face.

I couldn't really see how the machine drained body fat, but it was giving off considerable heat, so it had to be something to do with sweating, like a sauna. Shedding water weight is one thing, but fat? I wondered if it was healthy. Lori looked completely at peace.

After the 30 minutes was up, she stopped revolving and climbed out, bleary eyed. Steam billowed around her. She looked sensational, tanned and supple. You could see her abs and the muscles on her thighs and bum. It really had stripped the fat off her. She winked and made a face at me, as if to say, 'I told you so!' As she towelled herself off I felt like she enjoyed my eyes on her body.

'Wow,' I purred. 'Seeing is believing.'

I sat in reception while she dressed and Lori soon came striding out, in a dark blue business suit, invigorated and glowing.

'Next time you have to try it yourself.' She looked long into my eyes.

'Okay.'

'Do you need a lift home?'

'Please.'

I felt disorientated and estranged, like I needed space for a while. I had a lot to think about. As she drove me to my door I began to get the feeling that Lori Nasri was going to end up a very important person in my life.

The Eye Of
The Storm

AT home that evening I had something to eat and sat down, as I often do, to read boxing articles on the internet. On one site I visited regularly I saw a piece about Curtis and Ryan. It was saying they had been through the hardest careers in Sheffield, that no one had done them any favours and they had to battle for everything they achieved. I couldn't believe what I was reading! Those two were massive ticket sellers and had been looked after like babies.

Was it jealousy? I don't know. I shouldn't have let it bother me, but I can be hot-headed. One of the problems with the internet now is you can react badly to something and before you've had a chance to rethink it gets seen and reposted. I left a comment on the article. I wish I hadn't, but I did:

> My own career and that of many other boxers
> has been much harder than Curtis and Ryan's.

The Eye Of The Storm

They are looked on as the 'golden goose' and receive all sorts of preferential treatment. They get every opportunity going. We get ignored. You people don't know the half of it. Coldwell has pound notes in his eyes. He even stopped training the rest of us correctly once they came on the scene.

Within minutes my comment had gone viral and was being bounced around social media websites. It aroused a storm of controversy, with some people defending Dave, Ryan and Curtis and many others attacking them. There was nothing I could do about it. It was out there, so I composed myself and waited for the backlash. I knew it was coming.

About an hour later, my mobile phone rang. I sensed who it was before I even picked it up. Ryan had read my comment and he was furious.

'What the fuck are you on about Jerome?' he shouted. 'Giving it all that all over the fucking internet? If you got something to say, come down the gym and say it there. Don't put your dirty laundry out there for the world to stare at.'

'You know I don't train at Dave's anymore,' I said. I had recently moved gym to train with Ian Baines. 'I don't really feel like coming down there.'

In a way Ryan was right. I shouldn't have been so public, but I steadied myself and told him I had written it because it was true. That there were many others who really struggled to make any headway in the boxing world and were receiving no support, while guys like him got all the attention and glory.

'Fucking shut up!' he told me. 'You're just trying to get yourself some cheap publicity at my expense. We were mates and you treat me like that? You can go fuck yourself.'

Dave wasn't happy either. He phoned soon after. He agreed with Ryan. He said that I'd betrayed him.

'I've kept you going for years.' I could tell from his voice he was fuming. 'You haven't sold tickets from the beginning, I could have let you go, but I didn't. This won't make anything easier for you, you know.' That really pissed me off. I bit my tongue.

Curtis distanced himself from it all but I knew he was on their side too. In one go, I'd alienated three of my oldest friends in boxing. I'd only told the truth, but I'd told it in the wrong way.

Over the next couple of days it built into a major scandal. All the boxing websites were carrying stories about it and net forums were buzzing with debate. Everyone had something to say about the Coldwell camp bust-up.

I hoped the whole thing would calm down and be forgotten. Maybe it would have done too, but my brother, Marvin sent it all spiralling into madness. He was only trying to defend me, I suppose, but he really didn't help. Maybe he just had too much time on his hands.

Marvin used an image editing programme to alter a photo of two pigs having sex. He put Ryan's face on one of the pigs and Dave Coldwell's on the other.

The Dave pig was giving it to the Ryan one. As soon as it hit the web, it was bounced around a million times.

The Eye Of The Storm

Ryan didn't phone me again and I didn't want to phone him. That probably made it worse. You could see in his media interviews that he was getting more and more frustrated about having to defend himself. He did a video chat with one reporter where he suddenly said he was making a comeback. He wanted a fight for the vacant British light middleweight title.

When someone mentioned the pig picture to him, he visibly seethed, holding his rage inside. 'Look if Jerome Wilson has got a fucking problem with me, we can have it out in the ring,' he said, at last. I fixed my eyes on his through the screen. 'I'm not pussying around behind a keyboard like him.'

That was it. Words had been said and momentum created. A fight had been suggested and it was suddenly a fight in which there was huge public interest. From then I started getting random, threatening phone calls, husky voices in the middle of the night. There's some dodgy people connected to boxing.

They said I was wrong to do what I'd done, that I should watch my back. They threatened to kill my brother. It was a crazy atmosphere. Something had to be done to bring it to a close.

Strangely it was the new lady in my life, Lori Nasri who had a big part to play in making that happen.

So Near But So Far

EVERYONE has a vice don't they? Something they do for pleasure that probably isn't in their best interests. I very rarely drink. Drinking shrinks the brain. In fact I've only been drunk about five times in my life. I've never smoked and I've never taken drugs.

People say that's abnormal in today's world, but that's me. I've always cared about my health. I'm not perfect, though. I gamble.

A friend of mine introduced me to poker when I was about 20. I started playing free-entry tournaments where you win prizes. From there I became quite a good player and a regular in some Sheffield and Bradford casinos. I liked the whole concept of bluffing. It's just like boxing in some ways.

An opponent who raises and expects you to fold is just like the guy at the weigh-in who shouts a lot of abuse in your face and tries to intimidate you. What emotions you show are vital. The best reaction is stay calm, have a poker face, don't give him anything to encourage him. How you react can be the difference between victory or defeat.

In the casinos I'm the sort of player who can walk into a game, start with a £50 minimum bet and stand up a couple of hours later with a grand, maybe a grand and a half. Not every time, of course, but I won more than I lost. Michelle and a few other people had sometimes said that gambling would get me in trouble one day. I guess they were right. But not in the way they meant.

A few days after all the internet nonsense with Ryan, I was back at work. I had four clients during the day and Lori was the last of them. Although I found our last encounter a bit creepy, it was good to see her again. She smiled her little smile and asked how I was.

'I'm okay,' I sighed. 'I've been having some trouble with some friends and my manager. We've had a bit of a falling out.'

'I heard about that,' Lori replied. 'I saw some of the interviews. It seemed to get pretty nasty.' She leaned in close enough that I could feel her breath on my neck. 'I wouldn't worry about it though. I'm sure it'll all blow over soon enough.'

I backed away and got her on the treadmill to warm up. From there it was another decent session. We worked mainly on leg strength. Lori was a good listener and you could do some quite advanced stuff with her. At the end of the hour she reminded me of the weight loss treatment and my promise to try it out. I was hesitant but agreed.

I followed her in my car, nervous about getting in the pod. I didn't really need to lose much body fat, either, but as it was going to be an important part of our business model I felt I needed to experience it for myself. As we entered the building Lori reassured me that it was necessary.

I stripped down to my briefs and climbed in. Lori watched as the assistant closed the lid and switched it on. It was searingly hot in there, almost too hot to bear. As the machine began to turn, it soothed me somehow. It was a bizarre sensation, like being a kebab on a rotisserie, but very relaxing at the same time. I could feel the fat just dripping off.

When the treatment finished, after 30 minutes, I was in a kind of trance. The assistant helped me out and handed me a towel. I nearly fell down. I was so faint. He showed me to a bed for me to lie down for a few minutes.

Lori came over and began wiping my head with a flannel.

'Well?' she asked.

'I feel drained and weak, but it was good, really good. I can tell I've lost a lot of fat.'

When I felt settled enough to stand they put me on a scale. I'd lost three quarters of stone. My stomach was ripped to shreds. You could see every line and con tour of my six-pack. I turned to Lori. She was grinning.

'I need some food,' I said. She nodded.

I got dressed and we headed out of the clinic and down to the casino floor for a meal. The restaurant was modern, brightly lit, with huge landscape photographs on the walls. Directly in front of my eye line was a desert scene with a lone, camel-riding Bedouin surrounded by sand dunes.

I ordered steak, vegetables and a couple of bottles of water. With food came conversation. Lori explained that a key part of her business proposal was licensing the weight-loss pods in a way that meant they were affordable for ordinary working people. She had devised a plan to make that viable. The idea was that the pods would attract large numbers of customers. Then, when people realised how effective they were, they would continue to use our other services.

We finished our meals and shook hands. Nothing had been signed, but it felt concrete. I had a sense of anticipation for the future. Combined with my boxing, Lori's business could change my life.

Her face changed. 'I'm so sorry, Jerome, I've got to dash off,' she said. 'I've got a meeting to be at in 30 minutes.'

She paid the bill and disappeared, but I was in no rush. I still felt the effects of the weight pod and wanted more time to digest my meal. After the waiter cleared our table I headed into the casino area.

'I may as well play a few games,' I thought. It had been such a positive day and the time seemed right to try my luck.

The casino itself was a grand looking place, lots of polished wood and green felt. There was obviously some kind of promotion on. On a circular plinth in the middle of the floor sat a beautiful sports car, a curvy masterpiece in silver and black, spot-lit from above. It had a large gate-shaped front grille and was so low it looked like you'd have to lie down to drive it. I've got a Ford Focus. This was like something from a Bond movie, it really caught my eye.

Mounted on a display case next to it stood a two-metre, diamond encrusted, decorative sword. A little sign identified it as a replica of the Griffin Sword which historically had been presented to military leaders who had done great service to their country in time of conflict. It was an impressive looking piece.

I drooled over the car for a couple of minutes then headed over to the poker tables. For mid-afternoon it was fairly busy, too early in the day for the nocturnal hustlers to be out in force, but a handful of players were spread over three games. I sat at one, introduced myself and used my bankcard to buy £100 of chips.

There were three other players at the table; a middle-aged housewife who kept smiling to herself as if imagining a series of private jokes, a German guy with hairy-backed hands and chubby-faced youngster in a cheap suit. None of them were very good.

I played for a good hour and a half, won a few, lost a few and was pretty much back at where I started when something in my peripheral vision alerted me that I was being stared at from the bar. My stomach twisted instinctively. Something in my brain said 'danger' and I looked up from my cards. My senses had served me well. Ryan was there, dressed very smartly, a small drink in his hand.

He was staring and his eyes burrowed into mine from 30 metres. For what seemed like forever, I returned his gaze, then nodded to the croupier that I was leaving the game. I gathered my chips and headed over to the cashier.

My intention was simply to collect my money and leave, to avoid a scene, but as I headed back across the casino floor I suddenly felt giddy. I hadn't eaten enough to compensate for the weight pod draining my strength and the adrenaline of potential confrontation had sapped my last reserves of energy.

I found myself in the middle of the floor near the sports car again. I've thought of this moment a thousand times since, how I would change it if I could, but rather than risk keeling over in the middle of the casino, I leaned on the edge of the bonnet, just for a few seconds, to clear my head. Before I knew what was happening, Ryan was right in my face. He must have run over to confront me.

'Get the fuck off that car you cunt,' he said.

I didn't want any trouble.

'Just give me a minute,' My head bobbed.

Ryan was fuming. He looked like he was about to swing a fist but thought better of it, took three steps back, pulled his phone from his pocket and started snapping pictures of me sitting on the car. People turned to see what was happening.

A suited, middle-aged man came trotting over and put his hand on my shoulder. He had a huge security guard in tow and a voice like warm honey.

'Excuse me sir,' he said. 'But our board of directors have donated this car and sword to Mr Rhodes should he win back the British title. We sponsor his boxing career, you see, and have done for years. The last thing we would want is for it to get damaged and to have to bill you.'

Ryan stared me down. The security guy stepped forward. I allowed him to ease me off the bonnet.

The man spoke again.

'We think it would be in everybody's interests if you accepted a fight with Ryan for the British light middleweight title,' he said. 'Financially we can make it worth your while.'

From behind him Ryan started shouting, 'Take it! Take it you cunt! If we don't fight in the ring I can promise you we'll fight outside!'

Flecks of spit flew from his mouth. They sparkled under the casino lighting. I had a sense of destiny, like watching a film when you already know how it ends.

Reconciled With Dad

DENTON Hugh Wilson, my father, I wish he had never got caught up in this mess. Not that we had a regular father-son relationship. I'm not sure that's possible with a character like Dad, but the last thing I wanted was for him to come to any harm. We've not always been close and in truth, before the build-up to my last fight I hadn't spoken to him for six years.

Dad was born in Jamaica and lived there until the age of nine. Like a lot of Jamaican men who grew up in that culture, he liked to put himself around. He was a bit of a boy.

He met my Mum when she was 17. He was a youth worker and she was one of the 'youths'. He has actually fathered 18 kids with nine different women. They are the ones we know about anyway. He was cheating left, right and centre. He hurt a lot of feelings. We always used to make a joke of it – because Dad went to

Jamaica a lot, we wondered if he had more kids there too. I wouldn't put it past him.

He was a karate instructor when I was small, always very fit. With age he turned to natural bodybuilding. He was number one in England two years running and came fourth in the world in the over-50s category.

I used to copy the exercises I saw him doing. Every night, before going to sleep I'd do push-ups, sit-ups, chin-ups off the bunk bed. That's something that's stayed with me. Some of my half-brothers and sisters really can't stand him, but I never felt that strongly. Part of him will always be part of me, but we never really lived together, Dad, Mum, brother and sisters like a regular family. As a kid I rarely saw him.

When I was small and still idolised him, there was a time he was very ill. It was scary. The 'baby-mother' culture meant he hadn't known his own father, so he made it his business, as an adult, to go and find him. He went on several trips back to Jamaica, trying to track my Granddad down. Eventually he did meet him, but by then the old boy was dying of prostate cancer. It was a short-lived reunion.

When Dad returned to England, satisfied but emotional, he booked himself in for tests. It was fortunate he did. The results confirmed that he also had the disease and required urgent treatment. They caught it at an early stage which meant he was able to battle through and survive. He used to say, 'My father's death gave me life.' He's a great talker.

The whole thing inspired him to become a community champion for the Prostate Cancer UK charity. He travelled around the country, giving talks and raising awareness. Afro-Caribbean men are three times more likely to die of the disease so it's something they need to hear.

I've always admired the way Dad took something so bad and turned it into a positive, but I'd be lying if I said he was a good parent. He used to let us down so often when we were kids. He'd say to us, 'Yeah I'll come and pick you up and take you out, be ready at nine.' We'd be sitting at the window, all keyed up and then the phone would go.

'Sorry,' he'd say, 'something's come up, I'm in a meeting, I've got to go somewhere. I can't make it today. We'll have to leave it for another time.'

It happened so often. In the end it became the norm. It was a surprise when he did show up! Those are things you remember. He probably forgets, but I don't. As a kid they leave a permanent stain on your soul.

Mum worked so hard to support us all. She always did her best. She worked as a dinner lady then in a few different shops. It upset me how little dad helped.

By the time I was offered the fight with Ryan I'd only just made peace with the old man again after our latest bust-up. My trust in him was so fragile that it didn't take much for me to lose it. I blanked him for six whole years. As usual it was Marvin who'd patched things up. But perhaps that time, it would have been better for everyone if he hadn't.

After Ryan had confronted me at the casino, social media had gone crazy once more. People had filmed some of the fracas on their phones and posted bits online. I arrived home to a flurry of comments and messages. The hostility was getting to me. It was so stressful. I began to think that maybe the best thing to do was fight Ryan and be finished with it. The money would be useful, if nothing else.

The only thing that bothered me was the weight. My natural division was light welter. I had boxed up at light middle before, but hadn't enjoyed it and I knew from our sparring experiences that at 11st Ryan would have the advantage. After the weigh-in he would rehydrate and eat and probably put on six or seven pounds before the fight.

Among the avalanche of messages was an e-mail from Ryan's sponsor. He identified himself as Aaron Cornfeld of CI Ltd and requested that I attend a meeting the next evening to formally sign a contract. He explained that he had contacts on the board of control and there would be no problem getting the bout sanctioned, even though I'd be boxing out of my usual weight class and Ryan was coming out of retirement. He promised me a £10,000 purse.

Ten grand was a big incentive. I'd never made money like that before. I let that override any doubts and concerns and more-or-less decided I should do it. Almost as soon as that thought solidified in my mind, Dad phoned me. Such a strange coincidence, Dad hardly ever phoned me.

I explained everything to him and he told me he had seen some of the internet coverage.

'We may have had our differences, but you are my son and I've always got your back,' he said.

I found myself getting a bit emotional. 'He does love his kids,' I thought. 'He just has unusual ways of showing it.'

Reconciled With Dad

We agreed that he would come with me to the contract meeting the following night, to offer support. The hate continued to rage on my computer screen, but with dad behind me I somehow felt better. As we drove together to the meeting in my car, there was a heavy atmosphere. I felt like we were heading towards something big.

I still wonder now if they set the whole thing up for publicity, but when we walked through the entrance, Ryan was waiting, in a dark suit, with a crowd of about 50 people standing around. He approached me immediately, jabbing his finger and raising his voice. He repeated his threats from the previous evening.

'You better sign that contract!' he said. 'If you don't I'll come looking for you. I'll smash you and anyone else who gets in my way.'

A standard tactic of boxing promotion is to get one of the fighters to play the bad guy. I wondered if that's what he was doing. I knew we'd had our problems, but I'd never seen him like this.

'Come on, Ryan,' I began, noticing that again several people standing in the lobby were filming the scene on their phones. It had to be a stunt to hype the fight, surely? Dad shouldered his way past me, putting himself in the space between myself and Ryan. He had some balls, the old fella. Fifty-nine years old and trying to break up a row between two professional boxers.

'No one will threaten my son,' he said. 'If you want to do him harm, you deal with me first.'

Dad put a hand out against Ryan's chest. It wasn't really a shove, more a defensive gesture, a keep-your-distance-type move. But that kicked everything off.

Ryan looked over his shoulder and within a second three bouncers appeared. They grabbed Dad and dragged him away, gripping his torso and restricting his arms. He struggled like mad. His shirt was ripped off. They jostled him half-naked to the doors and threw him back out into the street.

'He needs to learn how to behave himself,' Ryan said.

'You've taken this too far. I've come to sign the contract, let's just do it so I can get out of here. This is madness.'

Ryan leaned towards me, face screwed up, 'I've taken this too far? You...'

He broke off as Dad came crashing back in, face twisted in blind rage. Dad threw himself at one of the security team who had manhandled him, elbowed him in the mouth and knocked him down. They were scrapping like hell. Before I had a chance to move the other two came along and dragged him away to a corner of the lobby where a small crowd gathered instantly. It all happened so fast. I felt like I was walking through syrup.

As I approached I heard screams and panicked voices. I pushed my way through the bodies of the onlookers to see Dad lying on the floor, in a semi-circle of rich, red blood. He had what appeared to be two stab wounds, one in his lower stomach and the other on his right ribcage. His face was ashen. He was gasping. A woman knelt next to him trying to stem the flow of bleeding.

I couldn't fathom what happened. The security men stood placidly. No one seemed to have a knife.

Within minutes an ambulance arrived and I travelled with dad to hospital. I held his hand. He was barely conscious and mumbling under his breath.

'I love you son,' he was saying. 'I love you. Talk to me. Say something.' Shame burned in me. I felt terrible for the long period of time when I had nothing to do with him. In his delirium he was reliving my refusal to communicate.

They rushed him to intensive care and put him on a respirator. One of his lungs had been punctured. There was a danger he would go into cardiac arrest. They stabilised him but he was still critical. No one could confirm whether he would make it through the night. After a few hours I was told by the doctors to go home and try to sleep. There was nothing I could do. I could return in the morning.

I nodded and stood up, taking one last look at my dying father. And I said nothing. My heart was too full for words.

No Turning Back

MY head fizzed on the drive home. It had been an insane few days. Sleep was impossible so I made a smoothie and checked my e-mail. Cornfeld had sent me a bunch of documents. He was clearly keen to get it all signed and sorted.

I printed off copies of each item and started reading through. Altogether there was a £10,000 purse earmarked for me, which would be my highest-ever earning from a contest. Another form required details of sponsorships to set up reciprocal agreements between the two sets of sponsors. My head wasn't right from the lack of sleep and all the aggravation. I just wanted everything done. Without informing Lori, I forged her signature on the document and used her company logo on it.

I knew this was wrong, but somehow felt I had no choice. I scanned and e-mailed it back to him, then crashed into some sort of twisted sleep and awoke a few hours later, slumped over the table next to the computer.

I went straight to visit Dad at the hospital. There had been no change in his condition. He was in and out of consciousness and on heavy drugs for the pain. I had never seen him look so vulnerable.

Around lunchtime I went back home. A multitude of messages clogged my phone. Among others, Lori had been trying to get in touch. I phoned her back, head fuzzy from tiredness.

'Hi Jerome,' she said. 'I've had a strange phone call. What do you know about a man called Aaron Cornfeld?'

Fuck! Obviously, as Lori's details were on the document, Ryan's promotional team had contacted her to make sure everything was legitimate.

I owned up and told her I had used her signature. Her tone instantly changed.

'Okay,' she said. 'I suspected as much. I just didn't think you were that sort of person.'

She sighed. 'Jerome, I informed them that I knew nothing about it.'

There was a pause. What happened to Dad had changed my attitude to the fight. I didn't want to see it jeopardised.

'Lori, I'm really sorry. I've had so much stress recently and I've not been myself. All this stuff with Ryan and my Dad, it's got me acting crazy.'

'How can we go into business together without trust? Everything's on hold for now,' she said. 'Meet me on Wednesday at 12 at Café Dorado to discuss it.' The line clicked dead.

For two days I lived in limbo. So did Dad. My whole family was on edge.

Café Dorado was a vegan place not far from Leopold Square in central Sheffield. It wasn't really my sort of place, full of students and hipsters, but we'd been there for coffee a few times after training. They burned incense in there, served bean burgers and played Mumford and Sons or Ed Sheeran on the stereo – stuff like that.

As soon as I walked in I saw her. There were a few tables of long-haired youngsters and then her, set apart in the corner in a trouser suit and blouse. She was stirring a cappuccino, staring at it intently. I approached, but she didn't look up.

'Lori,' I said, as I reached the table.

She raised her face. There were dark rings under her eyes and her hair was more untidy than usual. She swept some of it back over her head with a limp gesture.

'Are you okay?' I asked. I'd never seen her like this before. Her veneer of groomed professionalism had slipped. She reached out her hand, offering it to me as if she had no further use for it. I held it gently and sat on a chair opposite hers.

'I haven't been sleeping,' she said.

'Me neither.'

'I know, I heard about your Dad and everything that happened. I'm sorry, Jerome.'

'It's okay. I'm just going through a difficult time. It'll work itself out. It always does.'

'No really, Jerome. I'm sorry.' Her eyes were moist.

'What are you apologising for?'

'I feel terrible about this. I didn't know you'd end up being such a great guy. I enjoyed our training sessions so much but...'

Her voice trailed away. She looked back down at her drink, steaming gently on the table in front of her.

'Go on.'

'The truth is you've been manipulated. I feel awful, really. Until very recently I used to work for CI.'

'Who?'

'Creative Innovation Ltd. You know, Mr Cornfeld?'

'Ryan's sponsor?'

'That's right. They asked me to do one last job for them. As you know I'm setting up my own business and they provided me with seed money. Ryan was looking for a title fight and they were worried that at 37 he'd struggle. So they examined various angles. They hit on the idea of a local grudge-match against a less experienced opponent, a bit like a Rocky story. It would be easy to market and generate a lot of publicity. But there needed to be genuine bad feeling.'

I couldn't believe what I was hearing.

'So they employed a few people to look into different options. You were one of the options Jerome. Your manager Dave suggested you. He thought you'd be good enough to make a fight of it, but not quite good enough to win. He said it was worth the risk because you don't sell tickets anyway. As you're naturally much lighter than Ryan you'd be a good choice. I was employed to feel you out.'

She squeezed my hand a little tighter, as if she was scared I'd let it go.

'When I told them about your feelings of resentment towards Ryan and Curtis, it began to make sense. Then they triggered a chain of events to make the fight happen.'

'But the article on the internet?'

'One of their guys wrote that. We thought you'd probably see it. Obviously we didn't know exactly how you or your brother would react, but it all worked out better than expected.'

I half-heartedly tried to pull my hand away but she held on.

'The company?' I asked. 'Us as business partners?'

'That's all real.'

I was beginning to feel that real didn't mean much anymore.

'But I need the money from this fight Jerome. And so do you. We can use that as a platform to build on.'

'So you're not annoyed about me forging your signature.'

She sighed.

'Well yes. CI are still talking of making it a police matter. Let's see, but the important thing is the fight is signed, 12 September at Ice. I'm going to have some TV people I know working with you in the build-up. We're going to really push this thing and turn it into a national event. If you win, you're British champion.'

Despite everything, the thought made me smile.

'And if not, you still make good money.' She was smiling too then. She squeezed my hand and moved toward me. I sensed what was about to happen but for some reason didn't stop it.

'I care about you Jerome,' she said. Her lips pressed against mine. She kissed me. I didn't really kiss her back, but at the same time I didn't push her away.

She pulled away a little and traced circles with her finger on the back of my hand. I thought of Michelle and my kids. I thought of my dad and all his women and how his behaviour had hurt us so much. In that moment I hated myself.

I pulled my hand from hers. 'I have to go,' I said. Anguish churned my gut like sheets in a washing machine. I left.

Within an hour I learned that Dad had died in hospital.

The Best Of Enemies

THE funeral was a lively affair. If you have 18 kids it's guaranteed to be well attended. There were a hell of a lot of tears. My sister Nyeesha read the eulogy.

Despite all my issues with my father and his role in my childhood I was devastated and angrier than I had ever been in my life. The fighter in me took over. I wanted to hurt someone. I knew who that someone had to be.

At the wake after the service I informed my family that without question I would be going ahead with this fight with Ryan Rhodes. I bit back my emotion and told them what I would be fighting for. I felt I could avenge my father's death.

They were distressed by my decision, especially Mum and Michelle, but I had to do what I had to do. Mum thought I had taken the fight for all the wrong reasons. I consoled her and told her it would be okay.

By that point I wasn't going to let my family's concerns stand in my way. Too much had already happened for that. My mind was set on avenging my father's death, by fighting and beating Rhodes.

I made my way down to the gym to meet up with Ian, my trainer, the next morning. I had never felt so determined. My all-consuming goal was to win the British title and cause Ryan some serious pain.

I had always been a good trainer, but for this contest that was magnified. I enjoyed the challenge of putting my body through a punishing regime. Some don't, but I always loved it. Getting up early in the near-dark, running in the park, with frost on the ground, just you and the crows. There's poetry in that, as well as pain.

I always looked upon each fight as my greatest challenge, like a pinnacle I had to reach. If I hadn't pushed myself to the very limit, I would not be at the level I needed to be. For this one we worked on keeping my hands up, inside fighting and feet. I knew I would need quick, quick feet. In – bang, bang – and out – in out, in out.

I knew I would face that familiar second opponent in the ring – myself and this was the battle I most wanted to overcome. To banish that shy youth I once had been and bring my body and mind to some kind of greatness. It was the ultimate challenge.

Boxing is so very technical, such a hard thing to do well. As you try to conquer it, it overcomes you, becomes your identity. Without it, I felt I'd just be Jerome Wilson, bang average. You know, when Robin Williams is talking to the kids in *Dead*

Poet's Society and he keeps saying, 'Make your lives extraordinary.' That's how I felt. Boxing was my means to that end.

I didn't know what would happen, but I took all that motivation into training camp. I had 12 weeks to prepare for the biggest and most lucrative fight of my career. The camera crew were there. I blanked them and got on, two to three times a day, for 12 solid weeks. Running in the morning, strength and conditioning in the afternoon, sparring and pad work in between. Sleep, eat, train, repeat.

I hardly saw Michelle. She wasn't happy. She was starting to swell with our baby. She wanted more from me. She wanted the one thing I couldn't give, time.

I told her I was doing it for all of us, that if I pulled it off it would be the first step to securing our future and settling our family. Looking back, I don't know if that's really true. I had impulses to satisfy, needs within myself. Who was I really fighting for?

I lost track of days as I turned inward. By fight week I was in the greatest shape of my life. I had no doubt I would win. As always the last stages were about slowing down and recharging batteries. Before I knew it, I was at the weigh-in.

When I got to the Grosvenor casino I recognised a girl from the film crew, who I'd met while filming on *Total Wipeout*, a TV gameshow I appeared on a few years back, which gave me my nickname. She was a blonde, called Naomi, she seemed pleased to see me.

'Hi Jerome,' she said. 'We meet again!'

She told me that she would be doing a lot of the pre-fight promotional stuff, interviews, training segments, all that sort of thing. They were really giving this one the full treatment.

Myself and Ryan made weight. There was a strange, muted atmosphere until the stare-down. As we gazed into each other's eyes with cameras popping all around, it began to hit me. There was such hate. He had been my friend. They were calling the show 'The Best Of Enemies'.

I did my first interview shortly afterwards. Naomi was aware of our story and wanted to find out more about what had happened, and why this fight was taking place.

It began well enough. I told her a bit about the history between myself and Ryan. But as I explained things to her and described how the friendship had broken down I got a lump of emotion in my throat. The beginnings of tears formed in my eyes.

'Are you okay?' she asked. 'Do you want us to stop filming?'

The fight I had wanted for the last few weeks, due to all the anguish and nonsense suddenly seemed irrelevant.

In that moment I looked back at everything and saw it for what it was. Bullshit. Silly, macho egos and pride, friendships forged in sweat had been shattered. Life had been lost and for what?

I was openly crying at that point. I asked her not to use the recording. It was a day before the fight and I couldn't back out, but I had come through an intense emotional U-turn and realised I didn't want to fight Ryan. I dried my cheeks, got my game face back on and headed home.

In the car I spoke to Lori on the phone.

'I don't know any more,' I told her. 'I don't want this fight to go ahead. You should speak to your people, speak to Dave and pull the show.'

'We can't do that now,' she said.

'But my heart isn't in it. It doesn't feel right.'

Lori sounded disappointed in me.

'There's too much on it Jerome. And you've burnt your other bridges. You'll be sued for breach of contract and your career will be over. You'll be destroyed if this fight doesn't happen.'

I thought of Michelle and the kids. Lori was right. If I scratched out now, how would I provide for them in the future?

I felt saddened that it had come to this. When I got home I called Ian, to tell him how I was feeling.

'It might just be a bit of pre-fight nerves,' he said. 'It affects different people in different ways. But it's all come too far now to pull out now.'

I didn't feel like eating. I had a hot a bath and went to bed. I didn't feel tired, and didn't sleep well.

The morning of fight day, I woke up, had a good, porridge breakfast then watched a few boxing movies to get me in the mood. It was sunny, so afterwards I sat in the garden.

Every now and then Mum or my brother would wander out to see how I was.

Time flew and in an instant I was at the venue. There were six other supporting bouts before ours. It hadn't been easy but I tried to kid myself into the right frame of mind. I had a picture of our Dad, with me and Marvin as kids in my pocket for motivation.

While the building filled up with fans and the preliminaries got underway, I saw Michelle and Serenity. I made sure they were seated in a secure place so they could see the action, but not be in danger from the crowd. Once they were settled I made my way to the changing room.

On the walk down I was greeted by Naomi and the film crew. Seeing her again rekindled all my emotions from the day before. My state of mind wobbled. I mumbled something for the cameras, but inside I was screaming that I didn't want the fight to go ahead.

Time went so fast. The next thing I knew Dizzee was playing and the MC was calling my name. The crowd gave me a great reception. There was so much noise, it lifted me up, boosted my energy. Then I was in the ring, staring at Ryan.

That plan kept repeating itself in my mind – keep moving, don't stand and trade, keep him off guard, be smarter, be faster…

Views From Ringside

Michelle Boyce (Jerome's girlfriend)

When I first met Jerome he hadn't turned pro yet. He'd fought in the amateurs but he was just training and stuff. At the time he was more into the personal fitness work and that's how we got talking.

Before I knew him I used to watch boxing on the telly sometimes, but watching strangers on telly and watching your boyfriend do it live are completely different. When it was just me and him it wasn't so much of an issue, but once we started having children together I didn't like it. I thought it was quite a selfish thing to do when you've got a family.

He turned pro just after Serenity was born and it did cause problems between us. I didn't feel he committed as much to us as he did to the boxing. I felt like it took over everything. He had to train twice a day and then he was working as well and it meant we couldn't do much together as a family.

I always used to say to him, 'When you go in that ring, you're risking your life.' Everybody thinks it's not going to happen to them, but it does happen to some.

I always went to support him, though. There were only two fights I missed and that's because one was in Birmingham and one was in Manchester. Watching him from ringside never really fazed me. He always looked like he could manage himself in there. People used to say, 'How can you sit there and watch him,' but it never really fazed me until his last fight.

It was the most challenging fight of his career and the truth is I didn't want him to do it. Even beforehand I said, 'Please don't fight him. I've got a bad feeling and I don't want it to happen.'

I had a dream a few days before and I rang him up in the early hours of the morning and said, 'Don't do it. Please, don't do it.'

I dreamt the fight went badly and he ended up in a coma. But obviously I was pregnant at the time and I kept having funny dreams. One night I dreamt a young lad I know got stabbed and another night I dreamt about Jerome. In the dream, it was so clear, he was lying there in a coma and I kissed his head and said, 'Please don't leave me.' After that he recovered.

When I called and told him about the dream he said, 'Thanks babe, you've jinxed me now!' It's weird, looking back.

On the night itself I had such a heavy feeling of fear and worry. From the moment I got in the car to drive to the venue I was overcome with dread. On the way there I kept talking to Jerome on the phone. I tried to be encouraging but it was difficult. He could probably tell how anxious I was.

Probably the worst thing was that he'd asked for Serenity to be there. It was the first time she'd been and she was only three. I think Jerome knew what he was facing and wanted support.

Jerome's opponent walked out and he looked so mean. His back was huge. Once it started they were both really going hell for leather. I'd never really seen Jerome get properly hurt up until then. He might have had a little bit of blood on his nose or a scratch here and there but nothing more than that.

In the second he got put down. I couldn't take it anymore. He went face first to the floor. He might have wobbled a bit in the past, but nothing like that. I've never seen him hit like that.

That was enough for me. I was saying, 'They need to stop this fight.' But he got up and carried on, then it was only a matter of seconds before the round ended. I thought he might have a chance to sort himself out in the corner.

When he came back out for the third his legs still looked wobbly to me. He just didn't look right. I was shouting, 'You need to get him out of there, stop the fight. Please stop the fight!' I wanted his corner to throw in the towel.

Nobody was listening, they were just enjoying the excitement. That's fine, but when you love one of the fighters, that excitement is horrible. For the rest of the fight I was praying for the end. I couldn't wait for it to be over. I didn't care if he lost, I just wanted him to be okay.

I was trying to hide Serenity from what was going on at the same time. At the beginning, when they played his music and Jerome walked out she loved it, but once the fight started she got upset. She screwed up her face saying, 'I don't like it Mummy. What's Daddy doing? Is daddy okay?'

I was forcing myself to make her feel better, saying 'he's fine, he's fine'. After the second-round knockdown I just started covering her eyes because I couldn't even bear it, so God knows what it was like for her.

I was watching but not watching at the same time. It was awful. I didn't know what to do with myself. Anyway, the fourth and fifth he seemed to recover and boxed with more control, but I just knew the way he came out for the sixth that someone was going to get really hurt. It was all guns blazing. I kept asking my dad and Calvin how long was left and I was clinging on until the end, hoping and hoping. Then just when I thought he was going to make it, he was… down.

I passed Serenity to Calvin and ran as fast as I could to the ring. But it was really weird, because I was pregnant and the week before I'd been in hospital with a little scare, so I was trying not to stress myself. You know when you're running but it feels like you're not going anywhere? It was like that.

When I got there they were digging around in his mouth, trying to get his gum shield. I was crying my eyes out. One of the other boxers, Ross Burkinshaw, was sitting in the front row and he and his wife grabbed hold of me and pulled me away.

They were saying to me, 'It'll be all right, he'll get up in a minute, he'll get up in a minute.' We waited and waited, but he didn't. I followed the stretcher out of the back door, but only one person was allowed in the ambulance and that ended up being Marvin.

I didn't have a car with me. The ambulance left and I went back in to the ring area. It was chaos. I didn't know what to do, I had two kids with me, I was pregnant and my man had just been rushed to hospital. In the end someone offered me a lift.

The doctors told us he'd had a significant bleed and they weren't sure which way it was going to go. They said to prepare for the worst. It was three o'clock in the morning and Serenity was still there, running around. She didn't understand.

I went in to see him, before they transferred him for the surgery. He was on a ventilator and quite marked up. There were tubes everywhere. I spoke to him and kissed his head. Because I'd done that in my dream, I thought I should do it again. Leaving him there was one of the hardest things I've ever done. I feared I had given him a kiss goodbye.

Marvin Wilson (Jerome's brother)

The date of 12 September is forever stuck in my head. A week leading up to my brother's fight Jerome was 100 per cent focused and I had total confidence. If he stuck to the game plan and boxed to his strengths he would come out with a victory.

I could also sense tension from him. He knew he was in for the fight of his life. There was pressure. Winning this fight would open doors. He had plans he wanted to achieve.

I remember during the week Jerome asked me, 'Do you think I'm gonna win?' I joked, 'Of course! All you need to do is hit and get the fuck out of there!' We both laughed but what I was saying was true. If he boxed clever I thought he'd be fine but if he got into a war, anything could happen.

There was serious tension at the weigh-in. We were surprised by the weights, particularly that Jerome was one pound heavier. I wondered how that could work. His opponent must have dehydrated himself.

On the morning of the 12th, Jerome was very focused, so focused that he hardly spoke. I know he was thinking about the job in hand. I remained 100 per cent behind him, trying to motivate him, but I could see things were on his mind. Some people had negative thoughts and comments about the fight. Our mother had a strong feeling in her stomach she couldn't explain. I suppose it's normal for a mother to have those kind of feelings.

At one point in the morning Jerome said to me, 'A lot of people have said I shouldn't fight him.' I didn't want him to think like that.

'Don't be daft I know you will beat him,' I said.

On the way to the fight in my car we had a talk and at one point he just looked back at me and asked, 'Do you really think I can do this?'

I told him 'yes'.

'If anything bad happens tell everyone I love them,' he said. I was concerned at the amount of doubt in his mind. Jerome always used to lack confidence as a kid and it seemed he'd slipped back to that a bit. I wondered if he was coping with the pressure.

'Don't be stupid!' I replied, turned the music up and put my foot on the gas.

By fight time I was very nervous. Whenever Jerome fights I get in to my own zone and seem to think he can hear everything I'm saying. The contest was close until he got caught with a big shot and fell heavily. That was towards the end of round two.

We were all amazed how quickly he bounced up. It looked a bad knockdown but he really showed heart. After that he struggled for a bit before finding his feet again. Going into the last round I felt he needed a KO.

Jerome tried his very best, everyone could see that. He put it all out there, but he's better as a boxer than a brawler. He got a bit complacent, dropped his hands and took a big shot, with the back of his head hitting the canvas afterwards. I went into shock. I didn't know what I was doing. I rushed to ringside, praying he would just get back up.

The paramedics had to act quickly, carrying him out to the ambulance on a stretcher. It turned out there was a fault with the stretcher fixings. It wasn't clicking into place and wouldn't attach to the ambulance.

They took ten minutes trying to get Jerome into the ambulance. In that time I was trying my very best to keep him alert, shouting, 'Jerome wake up, everything's gonna be all right.'

I held his hand and every time he heard my voice he would react with a little squeeze. From that reaction, a message got back to the venue stating that Jerome was 'responsive'. The MC announced it to the audience.

The truth is that his only response was the squeezing of my hand, which was gradually getting weaker and weaker. After all the frustration of trying to get Jerome into the ambulance I heard the doctor from the British Boxing Board of Control (Dr Hassan) trying to phone Northern General Hospital but he couldn't get through. I don't know how I managed to stay so calm after seeing so many failings.

I said, 'Come on let's just go.' The paramedics ignored me. Dr Hassan then said, 'Yeah, he's right, let's go.'

We all sat in the waiting room praying for good news. Eventually a nurse came out and told us that Jerome's brain scan results were so bad he had to be rushed to the Royal Hallamshire Hospital for an immediate, emergency craniectomy.

They informed us what that meant and how serious the operation was. They explained that it was a life-saving procedure. Without it he would die and if the operation was not completely successful he would also die.

Again I was in a world of my own, hoping everything would be all right, just blind hope. I found myself having flashbacks of the fight, having flashbacks of us as little kids, then I came to the simple conclusion that he can't leave us now. It's not the right time. He just needs rest. I tried to remain positive, not only for me but for our family and friends.

Ian Baines (in Jerome's corner)

Jerome could be sensational in the gym. He was unbelievably fast. He could dig a bit too.

I trained him for his last three fights. There was something a bit funny going on with him and his manager and former trainer Dave (Coldwell). There was a lot of history there. I think the tension came down to business. That's how it works. I used to say to Jerome, 'Look, that's the way it is, he's not your friend. He's your manager.'

To be fair, boxing's a horrible business. There's so many people that say one thing but do another. People scheming behind each other's backs. I've always preferred working in amateur boxing. It's simple. You train, then turn up and fight. In the pros there's so much nonsense going on. As soon as you involve money it all gets corrupted. Jerome really struggled with all that.

Anyway, fights are not always made for the right reasons. Sometimes there's an ulterior motive to do with TV money or tickets or whatever, rather than what's in the fighter's best interests. But Jerome had the skills to do really well. I was confident if he used his speed and footwork he would win the fight. The thing with him was that he had tremendous ability but there were weaknesses too. When I first met him I said to him straight away, 'You're a two-round fighter.'

If you look at a lot of his early fights he'd look superb for two rounds then take his foot off the gas. He'd be coasting. He was good on the outside as well but didn't like it if someone got in close. I watched the film of him losing to Jay Morris. There was no way he should have lost to Morris with his ability. It was because Morris roughed him up and he didn't know what to do.

We sorted all that out straight away. I used to tell him he needed at least eight rounds at high intensity. His fitness and punch output shot up. He really worked hard in the gym. I've not worked with anyone who wanted it more.

As we developed that side of his game he'd have spars and other fighters would be raving about him. Before his last fight I had him sparring some heavier kids and he was giving and taking. The other lads were applauding him, giving him loads of respect, saying, 'Jerome, you're a warrior!' He loved all that and maybe that worked against him in the end.

Before that last one we had a clear game plan of boxing and moving, staying behind the jab. I told him, 'I don't care if it's a boring fight, you just do what you need to do. Make him miss and use your feet.'

But at the weigh in the day before, I'd never seen him like that. There'd been a lot of aggro in the build-up and there was such an atmosphere between the two of them. I've never seen Jerome so intense. I thought it was going to kick off there and then. We had to drag him away and it took him about ten minutes to calm down. I pretty much knew then that it wasn't going to be a jab-and-move fight.

That was Jerome's other issue. He got affected quite easily by psychological stuff. He was always an unusual guy for a fighter, very thoughtful and sensitive. Nav Mansouri who was a good mate of his, a training partner, used to say, 'Jerome's far too nice to box.' He'd laugh about it, 'He's the poshest black man I know!'

Jerome was always into philosophy and what-not and maybe he did think about things too deeply. Boxing's an instinctive sport. I've seen Jerome hurt a kid in sparring, wobble him, but then step off. You can admire that in a way, but in the ring you have to be ruthless. You need killer instinct. Jerome had all the skill but that side didn't come naturally.

By fight time so much bad blood had built up that the gameplan went out the window. It didn't matter what anybody said, he just committed himself and that was that.

In fairness, Glyn Rhodes in the other corner had his tactics too and you could argue it was just that their tactics worked better than ours, but between rounds I was giving Jerome a right telling off. He was pretty much going toe to toe and I was saying, 'What the fuck are you doing trading with him with your hands down? Get back to your fucking boxing and work behind the jab. Use your feet! You're not doing it!'

But once he got in there it was like he got taken over, the occasion and all the spite got to him.

After the knockdown at the end of the second round he came back to the corner. I asked him a few questions. 'How much do you want this?' 'Are you going to make it your fight?' Things like that, just to see how he was. He responded clearly.

I thought he got himself back into it. By the last I had him one down, but I still told him to go out, get his hands up and box. If he went for the KO I didn't think he'd manage it. He wasn't going to win the fight slugging with someone like that. Both fighters were knackered and were just swinging away. When it happened, at first I thought he'd get up, but then the longer it went on you start reflecting.

Should I have pulled him out? I don't think I could have. It was a hard fight but he was okay on his stool between rounds. I couldn't have justified throwing in the towel.

Everything afterwards has affected me very deeply. I can only watch the fight back so long. I've got a recording of it but every time I've watched it I switch it off at the beginning of the sixth. I don't want to relive that moment and how it made me feel.

Whenever I went in to see him at the hospital I was in floods of tears. I felt terrible. I wanted to be strong for all of them but it just broke me up.

I don't work pro corners any more. That was my last time. I don't want anything to do with it.

I'm still involved with the amateur game because that's a lot safer. The way I work, the fighters become my friends. I get close to them. Me and Jerome will always be friends. I don't know how I would have coped if it had come to the worst. To begin with at the hospital it wasn't even whether he'd live until tomorrow. It was hour by hour. No one knew if he would make it. What happened to him will stay with me for the rest of my life.

Andrew Clarke (television commentator)

It was a heavy, heavy knockdown. You can usually tell whether a fighter's going to get up again or not from the way he goes down. If his senses are still with him then he'll put out a glove, turn a leg or a hip, just do something to break his fall and make it easier to rise. But Jerome went straight on to his back and his head bounced off the canvas as I recall. I haven't watched it back.

Our immediate reaction in the commentary box was one of concern for Jerome as he was clearly hurt. Curtis Woodhouse was my co-commentator. Curtis knows Jerome well and I could sense the worry growing in him as the seriousness of the situation became more and more apparent.

Wiped Out? The Jerome Wilson Story

All the right procedures were in place so Jerome was swiftly taken to hospital and, after a lengthy delay while the ambulance returned, the show continued. It was a strange atmosphere. We didn't know how bad it was, nobody did, but I do remember thinking about the conversation I'd had with him on the phone just a few days prior to the fight. I was after some background on his story and we'd got on well, ending up having a good chat about our ambitions in boxing, the perils of being self-employed and just life in general really. He was full of optimism for the future and then just a few days later his livelihood and very nearly his life had been taken away from him.

I love boxing and I always will but I seriously doubt that there's a single person who earns a living, or a portion of their living, from it without stepping through the ropes who doesn't at some point encounter a situation that leaves them feeling very conflicted. I certainly did in the days following that fight.

Dave Coldwell (Jerome's manager)

Jerome didn't sell tickets and lost to Jay Morris, so he wasn't a guy that I could afford keep putting on. It's just the nature of the game, if you don't sell tickets things get harder. Really you need to get yourself out on the road to make money. That's how it works, but Jerome didn't want that.

I'd told him that I couldn't afford to put him on our bills anymore and he asked if he could sell the fight, could he still box on the show. Obviously if you want to move up the rankings you've got to box decent people. So yes, I thought it was tough match-up, but I thought

94

if Jerome stuck to his boxing, he'd win the fight and that's pretty much the way it went. Every time Jerome boxed he beat the kid up, but unfortunately he didn't stick to his boxing. Once Jerome started having a bit of success he forgot about his defence and had a tear-up.

Obviously it was a great fight for the fans, but it wasn't the sort of fight Jerome needed to have. That's what led to the ending, which was horrific. As I watched the fight unfold, my concentration was on Jerome and all the way to the end I still felt there were ways for him to win. If he was getting a pasting you'd think to yourself, 'Okay, pull him out,' but he wasn't. It was give and take all the way.

I was sat in the front row screaming, 'Box him! Just box him! Don't get involved!' He just wouldn't stick to it. Even through all of that I still thought he was ahead until the finish when he got tagged.

To begin with Jerome was moving, so even at that stage I wasn't thinking the worst-case scenario. I thought he would get his breath back and everything would be fine. But then time went on and it just seemed to drag. I remember thinking, 'Please get up mate. Please get up.'

I'd been through something similar not long ago because Kieran Farrell (suffered a subdural haematoma against Anthony Crolla in Manchester, in 2012) was one of mine. The thing with Kieran though was he admitted he'd been struggling with the weight and dehydrating himself and that can contribute. With Jerome there was nothing like that. He never needed to take drastic measures to make weight, he was a natural athlete and always in shape.

I would say all in all Jerome's injury was the worst experience of my life. We went through such a range of feelings. This fight was a window to get people talking about Jerome. Suddenly there was a chance for him to make an impact. But it went wrong and he got knocked out and he's rushed off to hospital. We were left in the venue, panicking. It was horrific.

After the show finished I was my way to the hospital to see him and I got a phone call saying he had a bleed on the brain and would need emergency surgery. I had to pull over by the side of the road for a minute, I was that shaken. From that point on I was terrified.

Going into that hospital was the hardest thing I've ever had to do. The worst bit was when the surgeon came in. He said it was a really bad bleed and we had to prepare for the worst. I'm an emotional guy anyway but I was in pieces then.

It took me a long time to get my head around it. I was in a bad spot for a while. My business partners handled things because I just didn't want to know about boxing.

Once Jerome was out of the coma I went to see him and the first thing he said was 'sorry'. That was horrible. It just broke me up.

Glyn Rhodes MBE (in the opposite corner)

I knew Jerome well. He's a lovely kid and he'd trained in my gym sometimes. I have to say I was surprised when the fight was made. As a manager and trainer myself I didn't understand it from their point of view.

When Coldwell got on the phone talking about the match-up happening I couldn't really believe it.

If I was looking after a kid like Jerome and bringing him along, I wouldn't have made that fight. It was all wrong for him. Why would you put a kid who's still developing in with someone who's likely to beat him?

Jerome was coming off a loss in the previous fight and if you were looking after him you'd match him up sensibly to get him back winning and rebuilding confidence before another dangerous one. In my opinion his management/promotional team were looking at the fact they had a new media deal and they wanted this fight to happen because they knew it would be a real battle, a cracking fight for the viewers. It would start off their new TV partnership with a belter. That was their motivation.

We were very confident in our corner and we felt like all the pressure was on Jerome. We went into the fight thinking, 'We're going to do this.'

Once the action started it swung back and forth. It was one of those fights where it was difficult to pick a winner. But we felt that the way our guy fought he could have continued like that for any number of rounds. With Jerome we felt he was getting more ragged as the fight went on. It was like when you turn a hosepipe and the water slows down, then it starts trickling, then it just turns to a drip. You could see that happening with Jerome. The longer the fight went on, the more it was taking out of him.

Jerome was having to force the fight and when you do that you tend to make mistakes. Both men were tired but it was affecting him more. I remember in the fifth Jerome took a few full-blooded shots and looked so weary. I thought to myself, 'They should think about stopping this.' His head was really getting bounced around.

My policy as a trainer is always to think, 'That's someone else's baby in there.' You've got to look out for the lads in the ring. By the middle of the fifth I was certain we were going to win and Jerome was getting weaker and weaker. He was really getting some bombs landed on him.

At the finish, it was the shots that hit him before he went down that really set him up. He was caught with a little volley and staggered back towards the ropes. It's easy to say with hindsight, but in an ideal world the fight would have got stopped then. You could see he was done for.

He came back off the ropes and he was just fighting on instinct. That's when he took the punches that finished him.

I jumped straight through the ropes to put him in the recovery position. I just did it without thinking, maybe because I've been involved in another tragedy. I was working Richie Wenton's corner in 1994 when he knocked out Bradley Stone for the British super bantamweight title. Stone had a similar injury to Jerome and died two days later in hospital. In the end they just switched his machine off.

As a fighter I was on the bill when Michael Watson suffered his injury against Chris Eubank in 1991, so I've seen this kind of thing a few times. That sort of scene does stay in your mind as a fighter, as a trainer, as a human being.

I run a gym here in Sheffield and I train kids to box here every night. How can I go to my gym and train a kid to box and speak to his parents, knowing that one day there's a chance that kid could be killed or badly disabled in a fight? It's gone through my mind many times, but I do believe boxing does more good than harm. Of course there are terrible risks, but there's so many positives that come out of it, especially for youngsters.

Since the Bradley Stone night I've always been on the over-cautious side. I'm one of these people that would rather see a fight stopped too early than too late. The way Jerome went down was terrible, he was completely limp and still taking more shots on the way. I just knew he needed help. So I shot across the ring. I got there before the ref and put him in the recovery position.

I don't know if the ref froze a bit, but it's one of those things. I know he might blame himself for what happened, it's natural to have those feelings, but he shouldn't do that. With boxing it's the nature of the beast and these things can happen. Everyone involved can wonder if they could have done something different.

It was a horrible scene. Jerome was lying there. People were shouting abuse. There was lot of stuff going off that shouldn't have been.

All of us on our side packed up and sneaked out of the venue from the back. There was so much hostility around and we thought we might get lynched if we went out the front. Everyone went home and then for some reason I just drove to the hospital.

It was a strange one, something I did spontaneously. I didn't know how Jerome's family would respond to me, obviously it was my fighter that had done that to him and it crossed my mind they might turn on me.

In the end his family were pleased I came and welcomed my support. I remember sitting in a waiting room with the chairman of the Board area council and Dave Coldwell. All that kept going through my mind was Bradley Stone. The doctors were saying they were doing all they could and he was going into surgery and all this. And I just kept thinking that sooner or later they'll turn the machine off and he'll die.

Alvin Finch (referee)

I spoke to Jerome when he was in hospital. He didn't know who I was. He didn't know what involvement I'd had in the fight. We tried to talk about it anyway.

When I look back on it, it was a hard fight. It was very even. I didn't think either fighter was any better than the other.

I remember when I arrived at the venue Curtis Woodhouse came over and said, 'Who's reffing the Wilson fight?'

I said, 'I am.'

He said, 'Oh, I'm really looking forward to that one. It's going to be a barnstormer.'

I was like, 'Oh flipping heck, I don't like the sound of that.' As a referee you don't look forward to those sort of contests, but in the end I don't think it was quite as crazy as everyone was expecting, until the finish obviously. I was expecting a bit more blood and thunder.

I didn't think the knockdown in the second round was that bad. Wilson went down face first and he took a shot, don't get me wrong, but I could tell by the way he reacted that he was all right. After that I thought he came back well.

I only had Jerome one point down at the time of the knockout and to be honest I had him winning that sixth round as well, so if the KO hadn't happened it would probably have ended up as a draw.

Obviously the way it finished you ask yourself a lot of questions, but I don't think I could have got in any quicker and changed anything. Both lads were dog tired. By that stage of the fight there wasn't much accuracy and I didn't expect there to be a finish. The punch that got him was just a wild hook, it could have missed by a mile or it could have landed. Unfortunately for Jerome, it landed.

I knew straight away he was gone. I knew he was knocked out. He was caught again on the way down, just a glancing blow but then his head really bounced off the canvas. I didn't count. There was no point.

There was an English title fight on after and that got delayed. We didn't know the full implications but we were told that he was on the ambulance and had given some sort of response. I drove all the way home, a 120-mile journey in tears. I got home about three o'clock in the morning and when I arrived I got a text from Ali Hayes who was the inspector on the night, saying that Jerome was going into theatre for an emergency operation and it was touch and go.

I got up for work the following morning, feeling like shit, not knowing what had happened. It wasn't easy at all. I got a lot of messages of support from other referees and that helped, but of course it was a big weight on my mind.

The board got in touch to say there was no blame but it wasn't easy for me to cope with. It was one of those things that can happen in boxing. Things like that have always happened occasionally. They will happen again. It's a risk we take, we all take. I took them. Everyone who gets in the ring takes them.

I was a professional myself and in 1987 I boxed a guy called Oliver Harrison in Manchester. It was my eighth fight and I was stopped in the third, suffering an orbital blow-out. Basically my eyeball was pushed in and down. I had to have my eye socket rebuilt at hospital and that was me finished in the pro game. I had 106 fights in my amateur career but just like that it was all over for me as a boxer. I was 21.

I've thought a great deal about Jerome. I know how lost I was after my injury. Boxing was my life from the age of nine years old. I had nothing else. What I experienced is nothing compared to what's happened to him. I'm not a believer but I prayed and prayed for that kid. I just hope he's okay and he comes through it all.

I didn't know if I'd ever referee again. I had to think very hard about that. I did a bit of soul searching and decided to get back on the horse.

What happened still plays on my mind. I've tried very hard not to let it affect my work but I do find myself thinking to jump in quickly now. Everybody was very supportive and said, 'Just act normally and do what you always did,' and I've tried to do that, but there's been one or two fights when someone's taking a couple of shots and the memories of that night come back to me, of course they do.

Will I ever get it out of mind? No, but I just have to learn to live with it. If I stop and close my eyes I can still see him lying there and I think to myself if I'd stepped in, I could have stopped it happening. Could I have done something different? Could I have got in there early? I know it's wrong of me to think like that, but I do.

Of course they were both swinging away and if I'd jumped in and stopped it early there would have been uproar. Look at Howard Foster and the stick he got for the first Froch v Groves fight. Hindsight is a wonderful thing, but what happened, happened and neither me nor anyone else can change it now.

Brinneth Catwell (Jerome's mother)

I didn't like the boxing. I never did. But it was something Jerome wanted to do so I supported him. I was always worried that something might happen. I've been to pretty much all of his fights though, even a lot of his amateur ones.

I was nervous from start to finish, every time. I couldn't wait until the bell went. I just wanted it over. I was always apprehensive. I just wanted him to go in there, do what he had to do and finish quick.

The last one, I really wasn't happy about it. I said it to him a few times. He knew I wasn't happy. Even on the day when he walked out of the door, he gave me a hug and kiss.

'I really don't like this fight,' I said.

He told me to be quiet.

His opponent was such a tough opponent and he knew it. I didn't know why he'd want to fight someone like that. He was putting himself in real danger and I didn't think it was worth it.

When he got knocked down in the second round I thought 'gosh'. But he got up and I thought he looked quite strong. Even to the last round he looked strong, but with a minute left he got knocked out.

I just shot to the front. I left all my bags and everything behind. I tried to climb over the barrier to get into inner ringside, then I saw a way through and ran to the ring. I managed to touch his leg. Glyn Rhodes got there and put him in the recovery position.

They put an oxygen mask over his face and somebody pushed me back. Marvin took me around the other side of the ring. I was sick in a bucket.

I went back around to the front and his opponent's girlfriend was cheering and shouting, 'Yes baby! That's the way to do it!' The silly bitch. It tore me in half. My boy was lying there and she was shouting like that.

So I took my glasses off. I was about to go and get her but one of the security guys bear-hugged me and said, 'you're not going anywhere.'

Funnily enough I saw him (the security guard) again a couple of months ago and I had to have a photograph with him and thank him because he probably saved me from getting locked up.

The whole time when he got stretchered out and taken to hospital was a bit of a blur. Marvin ended up going with Jerome in the ambulance because he was the calmest out of all of us. To be fair I thought once he got there the hospital staff did a brilliant job. I really can't fault them.

Sheffield Teaching Hospitals Scan Results

Patient Name: Jerome Leando Wilson

(CT HEAD) 12 Sep 2014, 23:21 – Acute subdural haematoma with a maximum depth of 5mm is shown throughout the surface of right cerebral hemisphere extending along the tentorium. Thin ridge of subdural haemorrhage is also shown within the left frontal region. Some inflammatory changes within left maxillary antrum.

(CT HEAD) 14 Sep 08:59 – Since the initial CT scan a right decompressive craniectomy has been performed and this has relieved the shift of the midline structures. The acute subdural haematoma overlying the right cerebral convexity has been evacuated, there is persisting high density blood within a parafalcine location and also tracking on to the superior surface of the tentorium. The latter is associated with a volume of blood extending into the middle cranial fossa.

(CT HEAD) 15 Sep 00:57 – The superficial right sided drain has been removed since the previous examination. There is a pressure monitoring device within the left frontal lobe. Normal size and position of the ventricular system. There is a mild degree of herniation of the right cerebral hemisphere towards the vortex of the craniectomy. This is unaltered. There is another small, thin acute subdural haematoma within the falx mainly posteriorly and over the tentorium.

(CT HEAD) 23 Sep 2014 09:48 – There has been minor herniation of the brain through the superior aspect of the craniectomy site. There has been a significant increase in the fluid collection surrounding the surface of the right cerebral hemisphere. No other new findings.

Summary: Mr Wilson is a 29-year-old gentleman admitted as an emergency on 13/9/14 after being knocked out in the sixth round of a boxing match. CT brain showed subdural haematoma with significant mass effect. 13/9/14 he had a decompressive craniectomy. Mr Wilson has his bone flap out and must wear a protective helmet at all times. He was ventilated until 21/9/14.

END OF REPORT

Part Two – New Life

'If the brain were so simple we could understand it, we would be so simple that we couldn't.'

Lyall Watson

Resurrection

EMERGING from a coma, I soon found out, is a bit like being born. People have the wrong idea. They think it's like being asleep, then waking up, but I wouldn't describe it that way at all.

I remember at some point hearing my sisters Nyeesha and Channelle talking to me.

'Wake up Jerome, wake up. Squeeze my hand if you can hear me.'

I squeezed.

'He's not responding. He can't hear.'

'Or maybe he can but he doesn't want us here.' There had been problems between us for years.

And then my mother. 'Oh come on, don't talk like that.'

I don't know how much time passed. The next voice I heard was Dad's.

'I love you son,' he was saying. 'I love you. Talk to me. Say something.'

It sent a jolt of fear through my chest. Dad was dead.

Resurrection

I slowly became aware of hands on my body, touching me on the face and the most private of places. Was I with the angels? I opened my eyes, but it was as if I hadn't. Darkness became whiteness, but there was nothing there. I closed them again and it all faded away.

The next time I sensed a presence, it was Michelle's. She was crying. I thought of her psychic visits. Was I dead?

'Please come back to me,' she was saying. 'We need you! Please!'

I felt shame for letting Lori kiss me. Did she know? I wanted to reach out, touch her and explain how sorry I was. More than anything I wanted her to be okay. Our baby! She was carrying our baby! The memory was like a switch being flicked, pumping electricity up my spine. I opened my eyes. Everything was white and blurred. My forehead shot through with pain. I closed them again.

Nearby a small bird flew repeatedly into a window. I couldn't see it, I just knew. The tapping of its beak and the fluttering of little wings made a rhythm. It slowed. The bird fell to the ground and lay still. Its guts were full of plastic. I was gone again.

At the beginning, that's how it was. In and out, out and in, there was little difference between unconsciousness and alertness, between death and near-death.

At one point I opened my eyes a crack and thought I saw Michelle, pale, frowning, looking down at me and holding my hand. I couldn't understand what she was saying. Everything was confusion. I felt heavy. It was as though my head had rocks on it. Among the fuzzy light and shapes there was an atmosphere of menace. Was I in trouble?

Another time I saw a TV screen with a picture of my daughter attached to it. Little Serenity, she had been at the show. I wanted to reach out and stroke the photo but I couldn't move at all, not even a finger.

I don't know what order these things happened in, but later I heard Michelle speak again.

'I won't leave you Jerome. I won't leave you. You've had an accident my love. You're in hospital.' She gripped my hand.

'Hospital?' I thought, 'I don't want to be in hospital. I've got things to do.'

Another time I felt that Mum was there.

'I love you son,' she was saying to me. 'Talk. Say "mum",' and then very slowly, 'Say "I – love – you – mum".'

I thought I said it, but no sound came out. She kept on pestering me.

'Say you love me Jerome. Speak to your Mum.'

Mum had been at the show too. The show?

Something connected in my head. I fought Ryan Rhodes. No! Ryan must have put me in hospital.

'Shit!' I thought. 'After all that.'

I felt so limp. I didn't want to think about fighting. Especially not against Ryan. It had always felt wrong. I just hadn't admitted it to myself until the end.

I realised there were tubes going in and out of my mouth and nose. A period of time passed which was unclear to me. People around me began to respond when I tried to speak. This told me I must at least be making sounds. None of it seemed real.

Resurrection

It was warm on the bed and I felt light, nearly formless, like I could just float away. I lay there having thoughts I couldn't express. Visitors came in I didn't even recognise. I tried to acknowledge them. I wanted them to feel good.

I had the need to go to the toilet, but it was hard to control. I felt sickened and ashamed of myself. I had bowel movements, and felt it under me on the bed, clinging to my backside and the tops of my legs. I passed urine and felt it dribble over my thighs or stomach. It was even happening with other people in the room. In my mind, it reconnected me to myself as a tiny baby, like a circle of life interrupted and returned to the start.

I waited for help, blind and defenceless. No one seemed to arrive.

'How long can this last?' I thought.

Blurred figures in white came to brush my teeth. They gave me bed baths and cleaned up my mess. Michelle would sit for ages, talk to me and cream my skin.

It all felt wrong, but I couldn't do anything about it. Having a stranger wipe your arse is humiliating.

Memories came back steadily. I thought about the build up to the fight with Ryan, what happened to my dad, my business arrangements with Lori. Then I questioned myself – Dad was here, in this place, wasn't he?

I understood nothing. It was simple, I thought. I had gone insane.

I remembered how I forged Lori's signature, breaking the law. At times I was sure I saw police officers nearby. It was obvious they had come to arrest me. I became frightened, unsure of what would happen.

On one occasion one of the police-like shapes went and spoke to the other people. One turned round and looked at me. I could make out a face, but no features. I had no idea what had been said, but continued to worry.

After a while my vision gained more definition, but everything was split. I'd look at a person and it was like they had four heads. Another period of time passed and an Indian nurse with a kindly voice told me that I had to have an X-ray. I still didn't know what was wrong.

Later Michelle was with me once more. Again I saw police moving around. I tried to tell Michelle how sorry I was for what I'd done, for everything, all the business with Lori, how the last thing I wanted to do was upset her or jeopardise our relationship. I asked her not to leave me. I begged her. I'm not sure if she understood. I tried to read her reaction but couldn't.

Then about five nurses came flying in like a SWAT team and took me off for the scan. They were shouting and bantering, pushing my hospital bed out of the ward and into the lift. It was crashing into the walls and making all kinds of noise. I was frightened.

We must have been in the X-Ray room for about ten minutes. When it was done they crashed and banged around again and wheeled me back up. They were all laughing.

I felt relief that the police never came to speak with me, but later on that day, while by myself, I heard two nurses having a conversation.

'He's not to be trusted, you know.'

'I've heard.'

'He's suspected of falsifying documents. Management have said to be careful with him. Don't leave any personal items lying around.'

Later on that day, the Indian nurse came back.

'It's the annual staff party tonight,' she said. 'The medical team are all going out. There will only be a small cover crew on duty. But you're quite stable now, so you should be okay.'

I was shocked by what she was saying. Is that normal for hospital workers? But there was nothing I could do.

The Indian nurse came again later. She had a lot of make-up on. She looked a bit like a cartoon.

'Would you like to come with us?' she asked. She smelled like she had been drinking already.

I didn't respond. I didn't understand. Was she making fun? She laughed and said they'd be back when the clubs had closed, to continue the party at the hospital.

For hours the ward was deadly quiet and I was alone in the dark. Sometimes I heard creaks or pitter-patter sounds like there were animals around. I felt very hot.

Sure enough, the staff stuck to their word and came back late. They had loads of booze. They fed me drinks through my feeding tubes danced around my bed. Some started jumping about, waving their hands, shouting. I had no idea what was going on.

The next morning I woke up on the floor. I lay there for a long while. It was uncomfortable. Eventually a doctor came in. For the first time since the fight I found I was able to communicate with someone and be understood.

I asked the doctor how I had fallen out of my] He looked at me seriously, but with a friendly expression.

'You didn't fall out of bed Jerome,' he said.

I looked around. I was lying back on the bed, but he hadn't lifted me up or put me in it. It was puzzling.

'Do you have any idea why you are here?' he asked.

'No not really,' I replied.

'You had a fight that ended very badly. You've had a serious brain injury and been through a major operation to save your life.'

'Really?' I asked.

'Yes, Jerome. Really. You've only just come out of a ten-day coma.'

'Wow,' I thought to myself.

'A feature of the sort of injury you have received is that the mind can play tricks on you. It's not an easy thing to predict, all patients are different, but as people recover from this kind of trauma some report that their senses deceive them. You might see, hear or feel things which are not really there. It can be difficult to deal with, I know, but it should settle down in time.'

I allowed this piece of information to sink in. It had pretty terrifying implications.

'So did all the nurses go out clubbing last night?' I asked.

He laughed.

'I shouldn't have thought so, no.'

Making Amends

THAT first conversation began a chain reaction in my head. I had injured my brain so I couldn't trust it. I might perceive things that weren't there. I would find it difficult not to believe them. I had to try to use logic. I had to think very carefully about everything I experienced.

Was it real or not? How could I be sure? Is anything real? Such things were not very clear to me at that moment.

One of my first realisations was that I must have imagined the stuff about defecating and urinating all over myself, although the truth wasn't much better.

In reality I had tubes up my penis and anus to remove bodily waste. I had a catheter fitted, so couldn't pee for myself. It was done automatically. Once I regained a bit of movement, if I needed the toilet they would put me in a harness. Then they'd hoist me up off the bed and place me on a commode so I could take a crap or piss. They'd be doing that and there'd be nurses and other people on the ward.

The humiliation was a bit too much for a guy like me. Mentally I was crumbling. What I was experiencing was real, I guess, although at the time I wasn't sure.

I kept talking to myself in the same self-motivational way I had in my old life, before a fight.

'It'll be okay. You just have to stay strong. You just have to believe in yourself.'

After four or five days I started to get some co-ordination back, but I still couldn't really see and it was so hard to stay awake. Around then I saw Dad again. He opened a door at the far end of my room, where there was another bed with another stricken man. People had huddled around him, thin people with grey faces. They looked up at dad in the doorway and he stood there, backlit from the lamp on my bedside table. It illuminated their eyes. Two women smiled. Another was weeping.

My father spread his arms wide like a crucifix and began to recite loudly from the Bible.

'He will wipe every tear from their eyes and death shall be no more, neither shall there be mourning, nor crying, nor pain anymore, for the former things have passed away. And he that sat upon the throne said, behold, I make all things new. I will give unto him that is a thirst of the fountain of the water of life freely.'

There were tears in my eyes. I had never heard him sound so magnificent. The people in the room howled and wailed. Then dad shut the door and returned to my side.

Around that time I also received a card from the old ladies I had met before the fight.

'From the three ladies that you saw at the weigh-in. We're hoping that you're well.'

I can't remember who read it to me, but it made me feel better.

Over the next couple of days I managed to have conversations with a few other people. Michelle was with me a lot. I started to get enough energy to sit up in bed for a while instead of always resting on pillows. On Sunday 28 September, 16 days after the fight, Michelle brought the kids in.

I was in my wheelchair, with the catheter attached and my feeding tube in my nose. I had my hard cap on to protect my head. I was so keen to see them, but little Serenity looked at me with a face full of fear, then hid behind her mother. She didn't want to come near me.

It was crushing, but I did my best to behave normally and make her happy. By the time they left I could barely keep my eyes open.

Soon after that the doctors said I would be moving to another floor as I was making good progress. They were moving me off Floor K, the critical ward, to Floor N which was for more stable patients. It's funny how something like that can give you a boost, but it really made me feel better about myself. 'Great news,' I thought.

We moved to the new ward and I started managing to stay awake for longer. There were three other patients there with me, John, Owen and Davey. John had suffered an infection after spinal surgery. He was in a great deal of pain and could only move slowly. They had linked him up to a machine which administered painkillers and antibiotics automatically.

Despite that he usually had a smile on his face and was easy to talk to.

Owen was diabetic and had suffered a stroke. He was always very needy and struggled to move, but he was so funny. He made me laugh every day. Davey had endured brain damage, like me. He couldn't see and had problems with co-ordination down the left side of his body.

Through them I began to appreciate, for the first time that I really had been lucky. All three were in similar or worse positions than myself and yet they rarely complained. Sometimes at night I could hear one of them crying.

One of those first nights on the ward I felt very uncomfortable – my back hurt, I was restless and hot. I called a nurse and asked her if I could go to the day room to watch TV instead. She helped me across the corridor, settled me on the sofa and brought a blanket and pillow to help me get comfortable.

There was some typical late-night rubbish on, *House Doctor* or something like that. I must have been really tired, because I managed to watch only a little of the programme and conked out almost instantly.

Sometime later I awoke to the sound of giggling nurses outside the door. I opened my eyes and the TV was showing some kind of porno film. The nurses must have thought I'd been lying there watching the sex channel. I guess I had laid on the remote control or something, but it was pretty awkward. They turned off the TV and one of the nurses helped me get back to bed.

Making Amends

Before I fell asleep again I heard one say to another, 'We have to watch that one, and he's only young.'

I was still getting lots and lots of visitors, which helped me stay strong. It made me realise how many friends and family I really have. It also brought to light who wasn't bothered, as people who I thought would come and visit me never did. One of those, which really surprised me, was Lori.

I felt a bit upset by that, but had bigger things on my mind. I expected she stayed away for the first few weeks because she knew Michelle would be around and it might be weird.

I really hoped she would come in because I wanted to straighten things out with her, tell her I was fully committed to Michelle and the kids but was still interested in her business idea.

Someone who did come was Dave. I was a little embarrassed to see him initially. It was the first time we'd been alone together since all the stupid stuff with the pig picture on the internet. We'd had our ups and downs but this was a man who I'd worked with since the age of 16. I felt terrible.

He came in smiling and took my hand. I was really moved. He didn't seem angry at all. I gripped back as well as I could.

'I'm really sorry about everything Dave,' I said. 'It all got out of hand. I didn't mean most of it. I didn't want things between us to be like that.'

He smiled and squeezed my fingers.

'What have you got to be sorry about? Don't be daft,' he said, shaking his head. 'Don't worry about anything. It doesn't matter. You just concentrate on getting yourself well. That's the only important thing right now.'

I could see in his eyes that he really meant it. I was a little shocked, but also grateful. In his position, I would still have been angry, I thought.

Not long after that Curtis came in too. It was so good to see him. He came striding in with a big grin on his face.

'I'm very sorry for what I said about you Curtis,' I told him. 'I was just confused and angry.'

He nodded and started talking about something else. He didn't seem upset in the slightest either. It really choked me up that everyone was so prepared to forget past problems and were trying to make me feel better. It showed the depth of their concern.

Those two conversations went as well as I could have hoped, but a couple of days later came one I hadn't expected. I was sitting up on my bed with Michelle and my brother Marvin beside me. Marvin had just asked if I fancied a game of cards when Ryan, of all people, walked in.

My girlfriend and brother both smiled and greeted him. Marvin went to shake his hand. I didn't know what had gone on while I had been in the coma, but it didn't feel right at all.

I gathered my mental strength, such as it was. I figured he must have felt bad because of the way things turned out. I asked everyone to leave us so I could speak to him privately. He sat down next to the bed and asked me how I felt.

'I'm sorry, Ryan. Really. I can't do anymore then say sorry to you. If I could I would.'

He was silent for a bit and his eyes searched mine, as if he was looking for answers.

'What are you apologising for?' he said, finally.

It seemed a strange question.

'For saying the things I said, and doing the things I did to make the fight. I'm really sorry Ryan. I shouldn't have done it.'

He looked puzzled and uncomfortable.

'Its okay mate,' he said, falteringly. 'Don't worry about it. It's all forgotten now.'

'Really?'

'Really.' He shook my hand warmly and asked how I had been getting on in hospital. He told me of all the support from the boxing world, the fundraising and publicity. He said not to worry about anything.

I really appreciated Ryan's visit. More than anything it was good to feel that we were friends again. He hadn't mentioned our fight at all and nor had I. Understandable, under the circumstances.

A day or two after, Dad came back. We spoke and held hands. He asked lots of questions about how I was coping. We talked about many things. I had a burning desire to ask him if he was dead or alive, so that I could begin to straighten things out in my own head, but I didn't want him to think I'd gone mad. I was deeply confused, but I didn't dare tell anyone about all the questions I had. People get sectioned for less. That was the last thing I needed.

Dad certainly seemed to be living and breathing in this new life of mine. I could touch him too. As he said his goodbyes, I began wondering if I would have to revise what I thought was true from the past as well as the present. If Dad hadn't really died in the lobby of that building, then there hadn't been a funeral, although I clearly remembered it. Had he even been there when Ryan had confronted me? Had I imagined everything connected to his death? Had my damaged brain created memories too?

I really did not have a clue. I tried to stay calm. I realised I couldn't do it on my own – like everything else at that time, I would need help to recover my identity.

Chinks In The Fabric

AS if I had been under a blanket then started to find peepholes in it. I began to pick up on moods of those around me. It soon became clear there had been serious problems between members of my family since the fight. Michelle was on one side and my Mum and sisters on the other. This wasn't a new thing, in some ways they had never got along, but it had a new intensity. Little comments were made around my bed. It bothered me.

I badgered Michelle continuously. She tried to placate me. She said it was trivial, unimportant. I kept on until she softened. When I could handle it she said she would tell me.

'You don't need any more stress on your head,' she said.

But I was straining to fit together the pieces of myself. I didn't need added confusion, I needed answers. I asked my mother, brother, and anyone what had been going on.

It was several more days before I found out, but it seemed that in the frantic aftermath of the fight, when so much was still unknown, my mother had emphasised to nurses that Michelle was only my girlfriend and not my wife. Legally this meant that after the operation, if I had been disabled or uncommunicative, I would have been sent home to my mother's place, not to my partner and kids. Legally Mum was my next of kin and had the right to decide.

Naturally Michelle felt belittled and angry. She was powerless to do anything about it, even though she knew it was not what I would have wanted.

I really felt for Michelle. She had been through so much already, was heavily pregnant and having to deal with all this, while trying to make sure the kids were well looked after. For two weeks she had lived with the prospect of losing me, even if I survived. It is horrible how something like this can create division among those you love. There was nothing I could do so did my best to put it out of my mind.

Since moving up to the new floor, I received constant visits from therapists and doctors. Experts in speech, dieticians, gastro-intestinal specialists and physiotherapists all took their turns by my bed. Every day a new doctor so-and-so from this or that department would appear.

They carried out memory, cognitive, and physical tests, to try to determine exactly what kind of help I needed. They fired questions at me.

'Who are you?'

'Where are you now?'

'What were you doing before you came here?'

It sometimes felt like an interrogation. I answered cautiously. I was wary.

Getting out of bed was impossible without help. I tried to stand with the help of two physiotherapists, one on each arm and was shocked how hard it was. A professional athlete who can't get to his feet? I actually ended up pulling a muscle. I never even got fully upright.

At least I tried and it gave me something to aim for. I was adamant that I would walk again in the future. I had felt something down there, some little sign of life. That's what I told myself anyway.

The speech and language therapist asked me to read out short paragraphs off an A4 sheet of paper. I had special glasses and prisms for my eyesight, which was still split and shaky. I did it, but found it tiring. It was like exercise, the more I tried, the better I seemed to get. After a week or so I was reading fairly normally again.

Other therapists timed and assessed me completing puzzles and easy quizzes. Put the shape in the right hole and that sort of thing. Some took more time than others.

After many failed attempts I finally managed to get myself upright, still with the help of two physios. The next stage after that was just to stand still by myself. To be able to balance, once I was up on my feet. It was difficult. I wobbled like I had just shipped a big uppercut, but managed, just about.

Days after that breakthrough I was instructed to shuffle my feet forward while holding on to the physios' arms for support. I managed that too and from there my confidence grew. Some sort of normal feeling crept back into my legs.

'You *will* do this,' I told myself. 'You'll walk again in no time.'

I devised my own exercises. I wasn't going to let a little thing like a craniectomy beat me. I pulled myself to the side of the bed to dangle my feet over the side of it and while holding on to the side rails of the bed I stood up, then sat back down. I did this in sets of three, like a gym exercise, standing up for as long as I could each time.

I progressed well. They were pleased. The next time the physios came, they thought that as I had managed to stand without help I should try walking around the ward for a couple of minutes. They disconnected my feeding tubes and I shuffled off with them dangling from my face like tentacles. My sight wasn't clear enough to navigate the room and I had to hold on to an arm to stop myself bumping into things or keeling over.

Still, I felt I was moving forwards. By happy accident a couple of days later I inadvertently pulled my feeding tube out in the shower. It hurt like hell to begin with, but I felt okay straight away and thought I would be able to eat. I still needed to be examined as they didn't want me choking but I immediately began rehab and training to eat unsupervised.

The very next morning they started me on solids again. After being tube-fed for such a long time caution was needed and I was served three squares a day, consisting of a bowl of blended baby-style mush. My favourite meal was beef casserole. It looked like diarrhoea.

I was told that I would have to stay on this diet for a few weeks, before I could be tested for food with more substance. There was a danger if they progressed me too quickly I would choke. Despite these little signs of progress, I still had to press a buzzer to call a nurse if I wanted to go anywhere, so I could be pushed around on a wheel chair with a bag of piss on the side, like a geriatric.

'This will not be forever,' I kept repeating. 'You'll be better soon.'

I had to retrain myself to feel the sensation to urinate, with the use of a tap. This was on a catheter, so each time I felt the urge I would switch the tap on my pipe and piss into it. As the days passed this progressed on to passing urine into a cardboard bottle, until I was fully in control again. I was finally able to have the catheter removed four weeks after coming out of the coma.

Physically at least, things were looking up.

Once Upon
A Time...

I STARTED reconstructing my memory with Marvin. I knew I could trust him and it seemed a sensible place to begin. He came in the day of my first attempt at standing up. Marvin was pleased that I'd given it a go and soon we were back at the bed, playing cards and talking. I didn't tell him how much I was struggling inside my mind, I didn't want to admit that, even to him. I just said I needed help remembering things. We started as far back as we could.

My earliest memory was playing football with him on the grass outside the Bowshaw View council flats in Batemoor, where we lived with Mum when we were small. I was four and he was three. It was a warm day. Mum watched us from the balcony.

We were always sporty, me and him, always competitive, even as toddlers. We had one of those cheap, plastic fly-away balls you could buy for 70p in

Marvin and I as toddlers with our football. We were always competitive, even then!

At Hazel Burrow nursery with Marvin, 1989

Myself and Marvin with Mum. Leather caps and bow ties were very fashionable in those days!

Myself and Marvin graduate together, December '07

About to dive at the Great Barrier Reef while travelling the world

Dad with some of his kids

With Michelle, my rock

Fighting fit

Evading a lunging right hand in my second pro fight, against Donchev. I always prided myself on my elusiveness

A happy moment, relaxing with my friend and sparring partner, Ryan Rhodes

Filming the gameshow *Total Wipeout* in Argentina in 2011

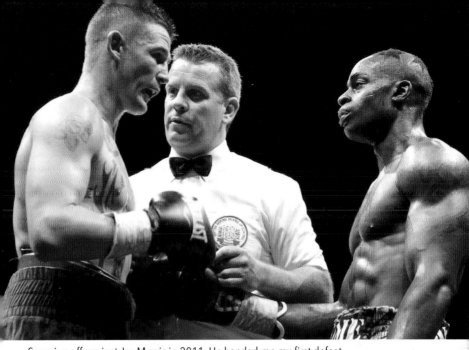

Squaring off against Jay Morris in 2011. He handed me my first defeat

Boxing Daniel Micallef in 2011

The aftermath of the best punch I ever threw and the end of Henry Janes's career

Sticking one on Sid Razak, in my eighth pro contest

I really enjoyed working with the young people at Coldwell Boxing. It was very rewarding

Myself and Ian Baines, in the dressing room at Ponds Forge, before the Mooney fight that never happened

I was more than ready for that Mooney fight. So disappointing!

Scoring with the jab after a long lay-off, against Billy Campbell

Campbell eats a big right hook

First fight with Serge Ambomo. My face says it all...

Speaking to Dave after the end of Wilson v Ambomo 1

Being interviewed with Dave by Coldwell TV after Wilson v Ambomo 1

Now that's what you call pre-fight condition! Weighing in at 10 stone 1...

Stare-down before Wilson v Ambomo 2

Ambomo 2. It was give and take all the way

At this moment, my old life ended and my new one began

The Kiss of Death

I don't know if it's possible to forgive these sorts of actions, but I want to try

Being stretchered out of the ring

In the coma

First visual scan of my head, post-op. The area of removed skull can be seen clearly

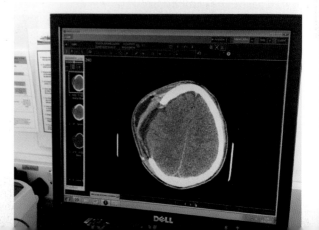

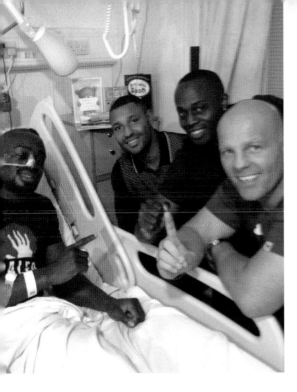

Kell Brook and Ryan Rhodes come to see how I am

Curtis visits in hospital

After my haircut

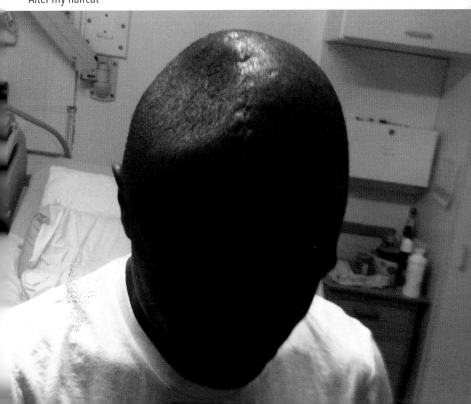

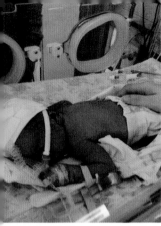

Cairo on the incubator

Visiting Santa with my protective hat on

Introducing myself to Cairo. Such a tiny baby!

With Serenity and Cairo, a few days after the birth

I wanted one last set of photos in my boxing gear before I put it away for good. Here I am with my beautiful family. I'm a fighter, remember

a corner shop. It would get blown around in the wind and you'd have to chase it. I was climbing the grassy bank by the building to get it back when an ice cream van turned up. We called out to Mum. She threw down some money and we bought 99 cones with a chocolate flake, ate them greedily, got ice cream everywhere, then went upstairs and she cleaned us up with tissues – so happy.

Marvin smiled and nodded. At least I had some memories I could believe in. By that point my ability to speak had returned, although it tired me out to talk a lot. I often had to repeat myself to be understood, which suggested I wasn't speaking very clearly.

Marvin told me how quiet I'd been as a youngster. 'Almost timid' was the phrase he used. I didn't remember it exactly like that, but I knew what he meant. I was never a loudmouth or one to go around looking for trouble. I always tried to be polite, to respect the feelings of others. If pushed I could lash out verbally, but rarely physically and my primary school years had passed without fuss.

He asked me if I remembered my first childhood girlfriend. I did, she was called Kelly and I had been 12 years old. Some of her friends approached me in the assembly hall at Newfield secondary school and told me she liked me. I was petrified! She was really pretty too.

Towards the end of my first year at Secondary we found out that Marvin wouldn't be attending the same school as me. He had been given a place at Abbeydale Grange. Mum wasn't happy and I ended up moving school to be with my brother.

We talked too about my only childhood scrap. It was when we were slightly older, 13 or 14. A kid across the road had been picking on Marvin and it had turned racist and a bit nasty, so I went and found him and rag-dolled him around a bit, pushed him over a wall. He left Marvin alone after that. It's funny, I knew I'd be stronger than the kid before we started. He was a bit bigger than me, but I didn't care. It wasn't even difficult.

I was rarely in trouble as a boy, which was unusual for lads in my area. I only had one run-in with the police, when I was about ten. My cousin Marlon and some friends decided to break in to a garage near my cousin's house and start up the motors on the cars. We weren't driving them around or anything, just revving the engines.

I heard police sirens and was saying to the other lads, 'The police are coming, the police are coming!' They wouldn't listen to me though.

I ran out and hid behind a bush. I watched from there as they all got arrested. I was shitting myself! My Aunty was only up the road, but I was scared to go back there. In the end the police turned up with my cousin in the car and told her what happened. She went mental! Mum made me wash the dishes at home for a couple of weeks as a punishment.

* * * * *

Mum was my next visitor on the ward. Talking about the past with Marvin had settled me down a lot, so I went through the same process with her.

We talked about the time when I was 11 and I'd been playing with Marvin and my half-brother Sheldon. Sheldon lived with Dad, but Dad was always bringing him around to Mum's place. He probably spent more time with us than he did at home. We had long moved out of the council estate by then and were living in the house on Lichford Road in central Sheffield where most of my childhood was spent. It wasn't a posh area, but much nicer than the old place. It was a proper house with its own garden, big enough for a family of five, which is what we had become.

The three of us had gone out to a field near the house and climbed a tree. I'd got pretty far up into the branches when one broke, and I fell to the ground. The impact knocked me out. Sheldon and Marvin carried me home.

I woke up dazed and saw a bone bulging, pushing my skin out on my right wrist. Mum called an ambulance straight away. They said I'd suffered a concussion and kept me for the weekend to observe me.

I was discharged on the Monday morning with a plaster-cast on my right arm and had to wear it for three months. At the time I was at Newfield School, my first year of secondary and was struggling. I was never a naturally academic kid. Later on, when I was much older, they diagnosed me with dyslexia but back then a lot of teachers thought I was lazy.

As we talked about all this, Mum sat next to me and smiled.

'You always found school hard,' she said. 'Do you remember Auntie M?'

I did, my mother's friend Marion. They were close and I saw so much of her I called her Auntie.

'Well Auntie M had a younger sister called Kirsty. She knew a teacher at your school…'

Her words sent me spinning back. This teacher had been horrible to me. She was overweight and pale and never smiled. She kept trying to force me to write with my bad arm, but I couldn't because of the plaster cast.

She then told me to use my left hand. I tried but it was impossible. So I refused. She got angry and shouted at me.

Every time I went to her lessons she would make me read to the class. I was very shy and used to stutter while reading aloud. The other kids would laugh and make comments. It was torture.

I thanked Mum – not for the happiness of the memory but because it was another I could trust. It helped me believe in myself and the world a bit more.

Others came and went in those first few weeks. Dad popped back in. I asked him if he had ever said prayers for anyone in another room since I'd been in hospital. He said he hadn't. I tried to ask him about the dispute with Ryan and his part in it, but he could see I was anxious and told me to get some rest.

My trainer Ian Baines came, my family became regulars. Marvin and my friend Barrington would sit and play hours of poker with me – it was a way of encouraging me to use my brain. I spoke with Marvin about Dad.

In my mind I recalled his heroics in my dispute with Ryan. That yes, we had our problems over the years, but he still showed his love. As I spoke with Marvin, more memories were highlighted. Things in the depth of my consciousness were brought back to the surface. It was almost as if I could feel things moving in my broken brain, the synapses reconnecting.

As a teenager I had lost my childhood admiration for him and begun to see the type of man he really was. His reality and his public face are very different. He never spent time with any of his 18 kids. He didn't support and guide us as a father should and he played many brothers and sisters against one another.

I remember one time he told my half-brother Denton, whose mother is white, that 'only his mixed race kids give him trouble'. I always thought that was such a shitty thing to do, playing the race card against your own son.

He mugged my mother off and treated most of his other baby-mothers really badly. He was selfish and egotistical. Who was my true father?

Marvin reminded me how Dad had always been an actor, not a famous one, but he played a wide variety of theatre roles over the years. He also has a huge collection of gold. He calls it an investment, his retirement fund. Sovereigns, chains, pieces of jewellery, he used to love wearing it too. Dad's always taken care of his appearance, been a bit flash. Even in his late 50s he still went out on the razzle. I think he'll always be like that.

He told us all when we were growing up that we could choose any piece of gold we wanted from the display cabinet at his house. He may well have ended up regretting saying that though. Eighteen kids equates to a hell of a lot of gold.

As their birthdays came along, my older siblings went and chose their pieces. Some of them sold theirs and pocketed the proceeds. I always thought that I would never sell mine and when my turn came it would have a special meaning. Eventually, when my 18th birthday arrived my father hurt me deeply. It might sound petty, but he did.

I wasn't given a choice at all. He posted a gold chain in an envelope through the letterbox. When I opened it a sick feeling rose in my throat. It was a small, thin woman's chain, one of the cheapest pieces he had. As I opened it and looked at it, I remembered all the other birthdays of mine that he'd missed when I was young. Anger rose inside me. I felt disrespected.

I went and found him at his house and gave it back. All the other feelings rose to the surface and this was the last straw. I told him if that was all he thought of me then I didn't want to know. We exchanged a few words and I walked out. I thought he would come looking for me to apologise or explain himself. But he didn't.

He let it drift. It was four years before I spoke to him again.

In that time my brother, Marvin turned 18 and he got to choose his present. He came home with a chain about an inch and a half wide. I guess dad felt bad about what happened with me and wanted to avoid a repeat, but that made me feel even worse.

In the end it was Marvin who patched things up between us. He's often the intermediary in family disputes. He kept telling me that Dad was asking how I was, that he wanted to see me. I bumped into the old man at a party eventually. We spoke and made our peace.

For most of my childhood I grew up with Marvin and didn't see my half-brothers and sisters very much. My mother looked after a few of them from time to time, as Dad would take his kids from their mothers and drop them off with my mum while he pursued his interests.

I loved seeing them, but I really didn't like the way Dad behaved. When he did come to my mother's house he'd sit in the same chair, be given cooked food, eat it, watch TV then nod off to sleep without communicating much.

As kids we had the feeling that we just weren't important to him. Sometimes I'd try to grab his attention. I'd jump on him and try to play fight with him.

I guess it was a way of getting closer. He would play along for a bit but it was never enough.

Of course there was tension between all Dad's women. He cheated on them constantly and as I grew older I became aware of this, noticing how close in age some of my siblings were. He didn't move from one relationship to another, like a serial monogamist. He often had two, three or four women on the go at the same time.

This made me furious inside. I've never heard him apologise to my mother or any of my other brothers and sisters' mothers. I guess it's just a cultural thing. He seems to think its okay to do what he did. I've never understood that attitude. Some of my siblings really hate him for it.

As all this solidified in my mind, it was both reassuring and confusing. This stuff was piled up in my memory, like old books covered in dust. I just had to pick them up, blow on them and they became clearer again. But contradictions were revealed. Was I right to have positive feelings towards Dad? In my old life he had basically been a good guy, hadn't he? Yet I had now accepted that he hadn't died trying to defend me against Ryan, that none of that had happened, so when I thought again, what had he done for me?

At the same time, I was getting used to receiving information that flew in the face of what I thought I knew. I lived in the moment and tried not to get too hung up about it. Did this really happen? Did I do that? All realities were possible. I accepted and rejected them equally.

On 1 October, nearly four weeks after my last fight, I was sitting up in bed and had just hit Marvin with a pair of aces, pre-flop. He watched as I gathered in my chips and said, 'I saw Serge the other day you know.'

'Serge?'

He looked puzzled.

'Yes man. Serge! Ambomo. Your opponent.'

I had fought Ambomo back in May in a crazy, crazy battle. We'd both been on the floor and really dished it out. I'd hardly been able to move for a couple of days afterwards. I bust my right hand and was sore all over.

Michelle had been quite worried after that one. She had to help me get in and out of my clothes for a couple of nights. I remember her buying me some special bath salts. The guy was like a tank, he just ploughed forward, unstoppable.

'What about him?'

Marvin was looking at me quizzically.

'Nothing. I didn't speak to him. I was on my way home from football and he was there on the street. It was the first time I'd seen him since the weigh-in.'

'What weigh-in?' Marvin didn't seem to be making much sense to me. He shook me gently by the shoulder.

'Come on Jerome,' he said. 'A couple of weeks back. Remember we saw him running on Sheffield Road the night before?'

An image formed in my head of the two of us in Marvin's car, laughing. We'd just seen my opponent on the pavement with his hood up, desperately trying to shed weight. I'd assumed the opponent was Ryan, but now, as Marvin spoke, it came back to me as if I were looking at a photograph. I sat up straight.

It wasn't Ryan Rhodes beneath that hood, with his blonde hair and blue eyes. It was a black face, a mean face, screwed up with effort.

I flipped to the weigh-in and the Grosvenor the next day, the stare-down on the stage in front of all those cameras and fans. Ambomo was the one glaring into my eyes, his face like a menacing tribal mask, his mohawk hair-do, his huge back. When I thought of the ring at the start of the fight I still saw Ryan there, but the rest of it? It was Serge.

My voice faltered as I spoke. I felt foolish.

'So Serge was my last opponent?'

'Yes,' Marvin said, concern on his face. 'Serge Ambomo did this to you.'

The Kiss Of Death

SINCE my new life had started I had been re-learning lots of things, but this piece of information was particularly tough to conjure with.

We both sat in silence for a little while. Then Marvin said, 'Are you okay?'

I nodded. 'Just a bit freaked out. I don't remember it, nothing at all. When I try to, there's something else there.'

'There was a lot of anger in the build-up,' he said. 'A lot of bad blood from the first fight, don't you remember all the online bullshit that was going on?'

I thought I did. Online bullshit? The pig picture and all that stuff. I doubted myself. Yet Marvin's certainty registered with something inside me too. Somehow I knew he was right.

His voice got quieter as he gave me a quick rundown on how the fight had transpired. I won the opening round with jab and feet, he knocked me down at the end of the second, I fought my way back into it before the hurly-burly of the last. Then he told me about the end.

'The thing is,' he said. 'There's been a huge fuss about it all. He knocked you out with a minute to go. Then he got down on the floor and kissed you on the head.'

'What?'

'After that he stood up and made a throat-cutting gesture at the audience. Everyone went crazy. He's been suspended by the board. Papers and TV have been full of it.'

I was stunned.

'It was fucking disgusting,' Marvin went on. 'What sort of a fighter behaves like that? It's just as well you came out of the coma or I'd be doing time for that cunt, I'm telling you. His girlfriend was there shouting and cheering while he was doing it, too.'

'Has he said anything about it since?'

'He's done a couple of interviews and made some public apologies but I dunno. A lot of people think he's just making the right noises so the board give him his licence back. His people have been in touch to say he wants to come and visit you in here. I don't think it's right though.'

I responded instinctively.

'Nor do I.'

We played cards a little longer but my mind drifted from the game. Marvin could see I was tiring. He left and I was alone with my thoughts – thoughts about Serge.

I'd first seen him three years ago. He'd come into Dave's gym to have a look around and trained there

139

for a couple of weeks. He looked a proper hardcase, intimidating and mean. He didn't say anything, but he had a right face on him, like he could just switch at a moment's notice.

We acknowledged each other but nothing more. His face and head were massive for his frame and he had huge arms and shoulders. I don't know what they feed them on out there in West Africa but there must have been something in his upbringing. He almost looked like something you see on National Geographic, like a statue carved out of Onyx.

He had his own story to tell, like all fighters. He was one of Cameroon's five-man boxing team at the 2012 Olympics who defected from the athletes' village and claimed asylum here in the UK. They said they were being threatened by high-ranking Cameroonian officials. After a few days, he resurfaced in Sheffield. He was granted the right to stay and turned professional a year later. His manager and trainer Glyn Rhodes got him a couple of sponsors but other than that he was flat broke. A real, old-fashioned fighter, living in a hostel, training hungry. You have to respect that.

Serge was a dangerous guy and everyone knew it. People used to say he looked like Mr T. Glyn once quipped, 'He's got muscles on muscles, that kid.' He was in a difficult situation though and I understood it better than most.

People knew he was tough, but because he had no background in this country he couldn't sell tickets. One of the worst things to be in boxing is a good fighter with no fans. 'Who needs him?' people would say. He wouldn't bring money to the promotion and would be a difficult opponent for anyone.

Glyn was on about putting him in the away corner, but no one would book him. If you've got a young lad selling a few hundred tickets you're not going to risk him with a ferocious African fighting for survival are you?

When Serge arrived in Yorkshire I had been a pro for two years and had a record of 7–1. I felt a bit sorry for him. It's not easy to make your way in the boxing world and I hoped he could make it work for himself and do well.

By the time Ambomo sorted his medicals, registration and turned pro, in early 2014, I was coming off the back of an 18-month lay-off. Our paths just intersected then. Maybe it was fate.

I thought about all of this in hospital for a couple of days. It's amazing how things beyond your control can change the course of your life. What if Serge hadn't been granted asylum? What if he hadn't chosen Sheffield but had moved to Manchester or Liverpool, or Cardiff? What if my own career had taken a different course? Then I would not have found myself with a hole in my head and a mess in my mind. The thought depressed me a bit. I tried not to dwell.

Two days after that conversation with Marvin, on 10 October at eight o'clock in the evening my phone went. I had only just started using it again. A brief image of a truck dumping old tyres in a desert flashed through my mind. The mess of tangled rubber stretched for miles. I looked at the screen, squinting through my glasses. It took me a while to focus enough to read it.

SERGE AMBOMO it said.

Hand shaking, I opened the message.

'Hi bro how are you?'

I couldn't bring myself to reply.

The Noble Art
And Me

IT was a Sunday and for the first time since becoming aware of my surroundings I spent much of the day alone. I had begun to use my phone, sending a few texts. Doctors suggested that if I felt able I should write down some thoughts. It would be therapeutic and stop me stewing on my misfortune. No one had spelled it out as such but I understood I would never box again. How could I? Maybe once I'd sorted myself out I could go into coaching, but in terms of getting in the ring I was finished.

The thought gave me a lump in my throat. Thirteen years I had been in the game. Since starting boxing with Dave when I was 16, I thought I would be involved with it forever. There was so much more I wanted to do with it.

Losing boxing was like a bereavement. I was grieving, so started to write about it as a way of coping. It would be good for my memory too.

I had always found boxing very lonely, the loneliest sport. It's a cliché but it's true. When you get up there, it's only you and him.

I still love it, deeply and unendingly. I know that's nuts. I guess it's like a bad relationship you just can't get out of. Even when you can't stand it and it's destructive and hurtful, after it breaks your heart you still go back. You can't help it.

After starting as a youngster and being told I had great ability, it took me a while to believe it. At the start I didn't trust what they were saying. I just thought they were talking crap, but in the end it got inside my head.

I've got long arms for my size and that's a big physiological advantage. I could tag guys when they were too far away to land their own shots. Hit and don't get hit. Bingo.

As I continued to develop, sparring with good fighters in the gym, I started to believe my coaches' words. With that, a magical transformation came over me as a character. I developed self-confidence. After the first few times sparring guys like Ryan, I really thought I might be able to do something, so I decided to stick with it no matter how hard it got. I told them I wanted to be carded, to climb between the ropes before an audience, to do it for real.

My first amateur bout I was 17 and full of nerves. It was in a working men's club and the thing that sticks most in my head was that the room thick with smoke. This was before they brought in the smoking ban and two thirds of the audience were chugging away on cigarettes. I couldn't stand it.

I felt relaxed beforehand, weighing in and hanging about in the changing rooms. A few of the other lads were only skinny, adolescent types and they made admiring comments about my physique. Then when the runner came in and said I needed to get gloved up, nervous tension got the better of me and I started to feel really weak. As I walked through the crowd it got worse. It took an eternity to get to the ring.

My opponent was a lanky white kid in pale blue shorts. By the time the bell went I was almost sick with nerves. All technique flew out of the window and I just went at him and threw as many shots as I could. It was basic instinct.

I lost that first one, on points and felt absolutely gutted. At the same time I was just glad it was over and done with. The funny thing was, back then, I never did any roadwork. Afterwards I told myself that I needed to improve my conditioning. I reckoned it would help to control my nerves.

That's what I mean when I talk about the fight that's going on inside the man. My opponent didn't really beat me on my amateur debut. Nerves beat me. If I couldn't master myself, I'd always lose.

Chris Smedley was in my corner. 'Don't worry about it,' he said. 'It's only the first one. You put too much pressure on yourself. Don't try to please others. Do it to please yourself. Keep at it, keep learning. You'll get a win next time.'

He could see that my new-found self-belief was fragile.

I had a little chat with myself later, is this really for me? I decided the answer was yes. I had fallen at the first hurdle, but wanted to get up and keep racing. Nothing's worse than a quitter.

As my amateur career went on I learned how hard i ɔ fit boxing around the rest of your life. I wanted to dedicate myself to it, there's so much to learn, but I was attending college at the same time and at the beginning I was still competing in my other sport, which was basketball. My biggest problem was money. Half the time I couldn't even afford to travel back and forth to the gym and pay my subs.

There were plenty of times I trained and I didn't pay. It was only a fiver a week but I was so skint that I usually didn't have it. My Mum had very little money. All I had was my EMA (Educational Maintenance Allowance) which was about £30 a week but I had to use that to travel to and from college, buy books and all that stuff.

Sometimes I would sneak into the gym and if Dave asked me I'd say, 'Oh I haven't got anything on me, I'll pay you next week…' Back then Dave and Chris were great, they let it slide all the time. They knew I was broke so they didn't hassle me too much for it. I really respected them for that. Most of the time I trained for free.

That's how it was when I was a youngster. Like many people I was struggling. It's not that I was starving or anything like that but the things that people do for enjoyment, like going to the cinema or going swimming, I didn't have that luxury. I had my friends in the area and we'd play basketball in the street and that kind of stuff. I was happy, but of course like loads of kids I dreamt about being in a situation where

I had the money to do whatever I wanted. How can I make that kind of life for myself? I would wonder.

The truth as well at the beginning is that although I loved boxing training, I found it very hard. I would finish in the gym and be absolutely knackered! I didn't have it in me to go out running and do roadwork as well. It took me a while to develop the drive and dedication you need to fight well. It's not just about throwing punches. You have to look after yourself in all ways, inside and out. In my early amateur days I was yet to understand that.

At the beginning Dave and I were so close. It was almost like a nephew-uncle relationship. I respected him a lot and tried to take every piece of advice he gave me on board. I learnt so much from him.

He was here, there and everywhere, going to different shows and events. He might not be famous to the average man on the street but on the British boxing scene he's quite a major player. Back then he had a dog called Ty and he hated to leave his house unattended and the dog alone. I loved that dog, soppy thing that it was, and used to help him out and house-sit for him when he was out. He had a big old TV and a Sky box and I'd sit there, watch the boxing and mind his dog for him on a Saturday night.

After my first few fights a dispute developed in the gym and Dave and Chris parted company. It was quite acrimonious and left us all in shock for a while. Like everyone else, I had a choice to make. To begin with I stayed with Dave.

Dave had been good to me but soon I began to feel unhappy around him. I don't know if he was embittered from the row but he seemed to change. I didn't like the way he spoke to me, or others. He talked down to me and was sarcastic a lot. I felt disrespected.

At that time he was also training my half-brother Curtis Hoey, who was really talented. He kept comparing the two of us, saying, 'you'll never do that as well as Curtis' and things like that. I think he thought it was motivational but it happened too much and really got on my nerves.

For a while I bit my tongue because of everything he'd done for me, but eventually it became unbearable. I made a decision, told Dave I was leaving and went to train with Chris. He remained my coach until the end of my amateur days. Curtis continued for a while but ended up packing it in, in the end. He wasn't happy with Dave either.

When I told Dave I was off I didn't say I where I was going to train. I thought that might start a major argument. I just said I wasn't happy and needed a change. He seemed genuinely upset at my decision and said he would reconsider the way he spoke and behaved. But by that point I had just had enough of it. I thought if stayed I might end up having a physical confrontation with him, which was the last thing I wanted. Perhaps I should have given it another chance, but I stuck to my guns.

By the time I made that change I was training more seriously. I put basketball on the back-burner and started running in the mornings. Boxing teaches you lessons as you go along. I learnt mine through being in tough fights. I became Yorkshire and Humberside champion and frequently represented Yorkshire in competitions. About eighteen fights into my amateur career we boxed a team from London and I fought future welterweight prizefighter winner Larry 'The Natural' Ekundayo. He's 9–0 as a pro now and all the pundits are tipping him for big things.

When I fought him he had been a national champion in Nigeria before moving to the UK and was considered a real hot prospect. The first round was even. He was a nice mover but there wasn't much on his punches. Then I tagged him hard in the second and wobbled him. The ref got between us and gave him a standing count. That's how it is in the amateurs. In the pros I could probably have finished him off, but the count gave him time to recover and he went on to beat me on points. It was a close one, but he took it.

Another time I boxed a kid in a nightclub in Blackpool and forgot my gum shield. One of my stable-mates from the gym was on the show too, so I borrowed his. It was disgusting! I gave it a wash, but it seemed slimy and didn't fit correctly. I couldn't stand having that thing in my mouth and that made me fight really aggressively.

I came out throwing combinations and got him almost straight away with a sweet right hand. He slumped straight down on the ropes and that was it. I'd knocked the kid out in 21 seconds.

I was absolutely elated and spat that horrible thing straight out of my mouth. Chris pulled me into the corner. 'See what happens when you let your shots go?' he said. It felt great. That was the first time I made the papers. The *Sheffield Star* ran a little piece about my performance.

Another time I fought over in Ireland for a Yorkshire select team. We all flew over on the plane and I shared with Sam 'Speedy' Sheedy. He's 15–0 as a pro and fighting for the English super welterweight title now. He thought I was mental because I was in the hotel room doing press-ups and sit-ups and everything the night before the fight. You're meant to rest but I had so much energy and I had to do something. My body called for it. I'd done that stuff since I was a kid and it was like a little ritual for me. It settled me down.

There was a ceremony with music and stuff before the weigh in and quite a big crowd in the place. It didn't phase me though. I'd had about 20 fights by then and felt relaxed going in. My opponent was decent and came to have to go, but I saw everything coming from miles away and kept moving, moving, then nailing him.

When I landed I could see in his face that he was hurt and that spurred me on even more. I saw him wince, heard him gasp and enjoyed it. As a fighter you learn to appreciate another man's pain.

It was just one of those days when everything felt right, like how I imagine it is to drive a precision race-car on a track. I was slipping shots and came over with a straight right hand, which put him flat on his back. The ref waved it off immediately. I knocked him out in round two and didn't put a foot wrong. Perfection.

I always felt the amateur referees didn't like the way I boxed, though. I was all movement and trickery and they seemed to have a problem with that. They'd say to me, 'Lift up your head, don't duck too low, put your hands up.' I used to get warnings and points deducted because of my style, which I never thought was fair. There were definitely a few fights where I should have got the victory but it wasn't given. That's another one of those things you have to get used to, another boxing lesson. In the end I had 25 amateur fights and won 15.

I only suffered one knockdown in all my amateur days and that was when I was ill. I was boxing in Barnsley and had a head cold. The fight was at light-middleweight as well. That was never the right division for me. Even that was just a flash knockdown.

I had a good chin. I've been in the ring with big guys and taken big punches. The hardest hitter I sparred was the former Commonwealth welterweight champ Denton Vassell. Not necessarily in terms of raw power but he was a really sharp puncher. He caught me around the ear and I felt like I was on a boat at sea for a few seconds. Sometimes, with guys like that, I might see stars for a little bit too, but I always recovered. My body just seemed to have that ability.

Most of us don't really know what we can do. We operate within ourselves at all times. As a boxer you get intimate knowledge of your limitations. Once you know them, you can try to expand them.

More than anything else what I learnt back then is that if you can do something in the gym, you can do it in a fight. Your body's gone through the motions, you've proved it. If I could, I would go back to the beginning with a more positive mindset. I developed it later, but at the start I was too full of doubt. We all have our weaknesses.

The way my amateur career had gone sowed the seed in my mind that maybe I could turn pro. I thought of how quickly I'd developed in my short time in the sport. If I continued learning and growing I felt sure I could make an impact. The time wasn't quite right yet, though.

Turning Over

'TURNING over'. It's the phrase used by boxing people for going professional. Some kids really have no other choice, its fighting or prison. I wasn't one of those.

It was never about money for me, although I suppose that was at the back of mind. I was idealistic. I clung to a cherished goal of making an extraordinary life.

Not long after my last amateur fight I finished a degree course in leisure management and had a little spell of re-evaluating what I wanted to do. I went to the job centre, looked at some options and an advisor recommended I work on a cruise ship as a fitness instructor. I could earn money and take a bit of time to think. It seemed a decent enough idea.

I travelled down to London for an interview at the Reebox gym in Canary Wharf. There were over 100 people going for it. We had to complete reading and writing tests and a face-to-face Q and A. I got through and was invited to the training centre in Southampton.

Within three weeks they passed me out and I was placed on a boat called the MS *Blackwatch*, operated by Fred Olson cruise lines. It had all happened very quickly.

For the first 14 days we toured the Mediterranean and then for four months the world. It was an amazing experience for a kid like me. I'd barely been out of Sheffield before. My only travels had been away days with the boxing team.

On 1 April we stopped off in Singapore for new passengers to board. As I was strolling on the deck, I saw some people walking on that I recognised. It was my old next door neighbours from Sheffield! A guy called Robert and his wife. I was staggered. There I was, halfway around the world and they pop up. We had a quick chat and I told them to come and see me, so once they'd unpacked in their cabin and got settled in, they came up to the gym. As it was April's Fools Day I had it in my head to play a little trick on my manager.

I told them to call down to the salon and pretend that I had collapsed, thinking my manager would come running, I could jump up and shout 'April Fool!' and everyone would crack up laughing. Unfortunately the salon team called the ship's nurse and she had been attending to someone who was genuinely ill. The nurse came up, expecting to find an emergency, only to encounter me with a silly grin on my face. She went mad.

'What have you done?' she yelled. 'You've pulled me away from a seriously ill patient, this will go much further.'

The nurse went off and told my manager who then took her turn to come up and tear strips off me. In the end I was called in to see the captain. There were suggestions I could be thrown off ship.

It could happen for serious breaches of discipline, they just told you to pack your bags, get off and make your own way home. I was shitting myself! How the hell would I get back to England from Singapore with no money? Luckily the captain was a regular up in the gym and we got on well. He saw the funny side to it, gave me a talking to and let me off.

Soon after we pitched up in India and I went for shore leave. Very few staff were allowed off at that port, so I went on my own, a little adventure. I got in a tuk-tuk, a kind of local taxi which I can only describe as a scooter with a hut around it. It was the most dangerous drive I've ever had in my life. The guy was flying around corners and weaving in and out of other traffic.

The vehicle was so unsteady and swaying one side to the other. I genuinely feared for my life. I got off, shaky as hell, went into a local restaurant and ordered some food. I had no idea what it was. It was all served on big leaves. The locals wouldn't leave me alone. People with no shoes and pleading faces, carrying sadness on their skins. They kept trying to beg off me.

You can grow up on a council estate like I did. But poverty doesn't mean anything until you see it somewhere like that. There were people asking me for money who looked like they hadn't eaten for days. It broke my heart.

As we journeyed on over the great blue, I began to think about what was important in life. Really, we have so little to complain about. We have all the opportunities we could wish for and it's up to us to make the most of them.

Working on the ship was cool but didn't feel like the kind of thing you could do forever. I was in my early 20s. Life stretched out in front of me – an ocean of options.

Alone at night in my cabin, my thoughts kept turning to boxing. It had got inside my mind like a tapeworm coiled in my cortex. I couldn't forget it.

As the ship toured exotic locations in the south Pacific and well-heeled guests came to use the gym, my head was filled with blood and snot and sweat. Strange as it sounds I lay in my cabin dreaming of steamy rooms full of fat drunks shouting nonsense, while I waged war under the lights. A fire burned inside me. I had to go back to it.

I sent some messages to Dave, testing the water. I said, 'Look I know what's happened has put a dampener on things, with me leaving your gym and going to Chris, but I've been thinking about turning pro and I'd like you to train and manage me. Is that a possibility?'

I was surprised, but Dave was really positive in his response. He encouraged me, told me he'd love to work with me. We had some sticky moments before, but if I wanted to turn pro I would need a top drawer manager and trainer. Dave really knew what he was doing. He had contacts and connections.

Immediately I started to dream of titles, of Michael Buffer calling my name. I wanted to be a champion, to make my family proud, to show all those people that said I could do it that they were right. 'If you believe in it, you can't fail,' I told myself.

Altogether I was on the ship for six months. When I came off I went straight to Chris's gym to pick up my training gear. I felt uncomfortable telling him that I was going back with Dave to join the pros. They still hated each other's guts. So I got my stuff and just left.

Later on I told Chris by text message and that's something I've always regretted. It was wrong and weak of me to do that. I should have spoken to his face. At the time he was just developing as a pro trainer, but he's ended training lots of guys and working with manager/promoter Dennis Hobson. Again, if things had been different I could have gone down that path. I sometimes wonder if that would have worked better for me.

When I look back on all that, I can hold my hands up and say I made mistakes. I was a young man who wanted to make good choices, but I angered Dave in the first place by leaving him to go with Chris, then I angered Chris by leaving him to go back to Dave. It was silly and it didn't do me any favours.

I wish I could say that Dave welcomed me back to his camp with open arms, but I didn't really feel that was the case. I often got the feeling there was a funny atmosphere between us. Sometimes I'd ask him if everything was okay and he'd say, 'Yes mate! Everything's great,' but his energy had definitely changed from before. I didn't feel we were friends anymore. He acted like we were, but I didn't feel it.

I got a job as a fitness instructor at Handsworth Grange Sports Centre and saved up enough money for medicals and pro registration, but was given no advice on how to manage my accounts or how to progress my boxing career. I was left to deal with all that myself, learning on the job.

I trained with Dave for six months, sparring with Ryan, Curtis, Kell and all the others. Kell was a tough guy to spar. He never took a backward step and when he had a bit of success he would really step up and try and dominate. This made the sparring more like a fight but I was fired up and dedicated.

There was a time my car broke down so rather than miss training I cycled. I was pedalling from my Mum's house in Sheffield to Dave's gym in Rotherham every day for training, 15 miles a day on the bike, as well as all my other stuff. That's how much I wanted it.

I hassled Dave continuously and once my debut date was agreed, I got my first taste of the boxing business. I thought Dave would sell me to the public, but it didn't work like that at all. I had to sell tickets myself to my friends and family. If I didn't, I couldn't fight. I managed to shift 50 for my debut, much less than I'd hoped for. It was soul destroying.

I was all over social media, posting about the show, inviting people to the event. Smiling and shaking hands with everyone I met. I was driving around to people's houses, collecting money, dropping tickets off. It felt like I was my own promoter! Even on the actual morning of the fight I sold about 15 and had to go here and there delivering them. It took my mind right off what I needed to do. So many people made up excuses at the last minute, as well. Out of my 18 brothers and sisters, only four came. It was disappointing but that's the way it goes. Most boxers will tell you a similar story.

I told Dave that I hadn't met my target because people let me down. He nodded slowly, his face flat. 'I always hear that one,' he said. I remember thinking it would get easier later. When I won the English or the British title, everyone would want to come and see me. People are attracted to success aren't they?

I did an interview with one of the boxing magazines. They asked how I was feeling and I told them that everything was great but I hated ticket selling. I said I didn't think it should be the boxers' responsibility to sell tickets and that the promoter should do it. The promoters are putting the show on and collecting the profit. The boxer's job should just be to train and fight. Dave read the article and went mad.

'You can't say stuff like that in the media!' he shouted. 'What do you think you're doing?' I thought I'd just expressed my opinion. I didn't realise he would be upset.

My debut took place on 28 February 2010, on a Sunday afternoon show at the Magna Centre in Rotherham, one of Dave's regular venues. He said he'd organise a decent opponent but he couldn't confirm who it was until a couple of weeks before the fight. In the end he booked in a guy called Johnny Greaves, from east London, a proper journeyman. When he fought me he'd had 46 fights and only won two.

Dave called the show 'Repeat or Revenge' because Curtis was top of the bill in a rematch with Jay Morris who'd beaten him the previous year. Every fight on the card featured one of Dave's stable, Daniel Thorpe, Nav Mansouri and Chad Gaynor were all boxing. Being in the dressing room was like being in the gym.

Warming up beforehand with Dave I felt the nerves from my early amateur career come back. It was my pro debut and I wanted it to go well. I had to be careful not to put too much pressure on myself.

'You'll be fine,' I said in my head as I threw my hands. 'Box to your strengths, stay mobile.'

Dave sat me down and spoke to me.

'Don't think he's a mug,' he said. 'You're still learning how the game works. He can fight a bit, don't worry about that. Don't let his record fool you. Now listen – don't go for the knockout, that'll just piss him off. Show him a bit of respect, but keep busy with your jab. The main thing is not to give him anything to encourage him. He's not a pushover, he's an away corner boxer, he fights nearly every week and what he really wants to do is come through the fight unharmed. If you're nice and sharp, show him you mean business, he'll go into his shell and cover up.'

I came out to a speed garage track with a bunch of MCs rapping all over it. It was a real buzzy ring-walk. Dave hated it. He couldn't stand that type of music. I just had shorts and a black poncho on, Tyson style. I didn't want a silky gown.

Greaves' character soon displayed itself. If I hadn't been fighting him, I'd have been laughing. He was doing all sorts of things to unsettle me. He got me in a clinch, like a headlock and hit me on the back of the head. He was holding me with one hand and hitting with the other, spinning around, making faces. In the third round he started doing a little dance. I thought, 'What's this guy on?'

I hit him with some big shots and none of them bothered him one bit. He kept getting in my ear and going, 'Come on then, is that all you got? My granny hits harder than you.' I knew what he was trying to do, so I stuck to my gameplan and just boxed.

When the final bell rang I knew I'd won. I felt like I could have done more, but I didn't want or need to. They gave it to me on a wide points decision.

Greaves came over to congratulate me.

'Well done, son. You done well,' he said. 'You could be good. You just need to relax a little bit more.' I thanked him for that. I made him about right.

Afterwards in the dressing room, Dave gave me my money; £560 for six rounds of fighting, six months of training and weeks of hassle flogging tickets. My opponent had sold nothing and lost handily, but he got £1,100, double my purse. That was my welcome to professional boxing.

Despite all that I couldn't wait to get back in the ring. Having my hands raised and my name read out gave me a taste of what I'd always wanted. I went for a Chinese meal with about 20 family and friends to celebrate, feeling that I'd started. I'd climbed the first step.

Showbusiness
With Blood

IF you go into the fight game with a sporting attitude, thinking that talent will shine through, your illusions get shattered fast. I quickly discovered that boxing promotion, like a theatre boss scheming for 'bums on seats', worked on the basis of marketability first, ability second. Dave was pleased I got the win against Greaves, but he wasn't bowled over by the number of tickets I had done.

He congratulated me on the performance but over the next few weeks he made several comments about 'putting myself out there' and 'needing to shift a few more'.

'I know people,' I explained, 'but loads of them said they would come and then didn't. I can't put my hand in their pocket and take money out, can I? It's out of my control.'

Dave laughed it off and made jokes out of it, but I got the impression that it bothered him.

I thought it had been a decent start and hoped the more fights I had, the more it would pick up, but I was never one of those who was attached to a big social scene. I had friends but wasn't brash and loud. Those are the guys that sell tickets, the popular guys. I wasn't one of them and never had been. I don't like cliques and I avoid them. As a fighter, that's a bit of a problem.

An obvious thing to do, which a lot of boxers go for, is to attach yourself to a football team. Being from Sheffield I could have said that I was Wednesday or United, worn the team shirt to the ring, had the club badge on my shorts and I could probably have gathered some support like that. But I didn't want to be fake. The truth was I had never been bothered about football.

I hoped people would see me fight and appreciate it, that I would get fans that way. But in reality it just doesn't work like that. I was naïve.

My next contest took place two months later against the Bulgarian journeyman Danny Donchev. This time I found the ticket selling even harder. Dave asked me how I was getting on a few days before. I'd only shifted about 40.

'Is that it?' he said. For a moment he almost looked a bit angry. 'You don't understand how much money I'll be losing on you!'

Donchev looked big and strong. He didn't speak English much so there wasn't any communication. I remembered Greaves's advice after my first fight and tried to let all the tension out of my body before I climbed between the ropes.

I got in there feeling ready and let my combinations go, digging in with some really nice body shots. I could tell he was feeling them. In the second round I caught him a beauty, right under the ribs and he went down on one knee, puffing and gasping, put one hand up and started shouting, 'Emergency, emergency, paramedic!'

It was bizarre. I was actually standing in the neutral corner laughing. I'd never seen anything like it in a fight before. Anyway the referee stopped counting and waved it off.

They recorded it as a retirement which really annoyed me because I'd been busting him up. In my eyes it was a stoppage, pure and simple. When people look up that fight it should say Jerome Wilson W TKO2. They came out with some crap about a spasm in his back, but it's funny how he suddenly got a spasm when I connected with a right hand. The truth is I picked my shots and took him out. I reckon he was winded.

I had to wait five months for my next one, in September 2010, on another of Dave's shows at the Magna Centre in Rotherham. I'd been pencilled in for a different show in the meantime but there'd been a change to the line-up and my bout got cancelled, leaving quite a long delay for someone at that stage of their career. I was up against a guy called Phil Boyle from Middlesborough. Boyle came to win and gave it a go but I was too quick and sharp for him. I jabbed his head off and won every round.

A little while after that, Dave pulled me to one side at the gym. He had his fingers in so many pies. Among his various roles he was head of boxing for Hayemaker promotions and the man himself, David Haye, was about to defend his WBA world heavyweight title against Audley Harrison at the MEN Arena in Manchester.

What Dave told me was music to my ears. He offered me a slot on the undercard. I wouldn't need to sell tickets and it was a guaranteed wage of £1,500 with an overnight stay in a posh hotel. I was made up and ensured I trained as hard as I possibly could.

I probably didn't manage my diet as well as I should have done though. I was still learning and ended up having trouble making ten stone towards the end, so for a few days before I was going for long runs with my sweatsuit on and spending hours on the stationary bike in the gym.

The weigh in was huge event, with cameras all over the place and the guys from Sky TV filming. I saw my opponent, a Welshman called Henry Janes. He had some good names on his record, Kevin Mitchell, Derry Matthews, but he didn't look like much. He only looked half fit, in truth. I had a feeling I could take him apart.

The room in the hotel was fantastic and I remember thinking, 'This is how it should be!' I felt looked after, like everything was going in the right direction for me. That feeling was enhanced by the fight.

I came straight out at first bell and caught him with three unanswered jabs in the centre of the ring, then chucked the right hand over the top. It only glanced the top of his head but it staggered him. As he tottered away, I advanced, sensing the kill. We were only ten seconds in.

Wiped Out? The Jerome Wilson Story

I stood him up with a sharp left hook then speared him in the ribs with a long right. I felt so alert and super, super sharp. It was just target practice, I couldn't miss.

Janes had a go back and clipped me with a few glancing shots as I pursued him, but I was so zoned in I didn't care. I hammered away to head and body until halfway through the round I set him up with a jab that split his guard, then followed up with a straight right.

It was the best timed punch I ever threw. It spun him around and he landed face down on the canvas, like he had just been taken out by a sniper in the audience. In an instant I knew that was it.

He lay still. His legs were crossed over each other. For a moment, time stopped.

I stood over him, then retreated warily. A few more seconds passed. He still didn't move. Worry started to wash over me. My shoulders twitched as I watched him, hoping for a sign of life.

Dave towelled me off. 'Keep calm, don't jump up, wait to see how he is,' he said. But he didn't need to. I was genuinely concerned.

You get so focused as a fighter that sometimes you almost forget how you and your opponent are both human. I didn't know anything about him but as Janes lay there motionless, it flashed through my head that he probably had a girlfriend or wife, a mother, maybe even kids. They'd be horrified by what was going on. You don't think like that when you're swapping punches.

The ref put Janes in the recovery position and the paramedics came in to attend to him. It seemed like

166

forever but after 20 seconds he opened his eyes and began talking. He was okay. What a relief!

Once they'd got him back on his stool I went over and asked him if he was all right. He was glazed over. His voice was thick. He didn't sound as if he was speaking English, like someone who's recovering from local anaesthetic at the dentist.

'He'll be fine,' I thought, patted him on the back and returned to my corner.

Dave and I were both elated. There were 20,000 people and TV cameras in the arena and I had just scored a spectacular first-round KO. My record was now 4-0 with two stoppage wins. It had been a successful trip.

The crowd went crazy as I left the ring. Even some of the security guards were cheering. 'I've never seen a knockout like that before!' one said.

'This is how it feels,' I thought, as the adulation came from all sides.

There are always at least two stories in every fight though. While I went away and celebrated my win, Henry Janes just went away. That KO was enough for him. He never fought again.

They showed the finish on *Ringside* on Sky Sports and I got a lot of attention for the next week or two. Suddenly everyone seemed interested in me. I thought that this could be my opportunity to make my name, to develop some fame and sell more tickets. That's when I hit on the idea to go on *Total Wipeout*, an obstacle course type game show on TV. My kids loved watching it and I thought it would be good exposure.

I made a Twitter account with the name 'Wipeout Wilson' and filled in the application form. The producers liked my application and invited me for an audition. Although I made the final stage I didn't get through. Then I reapplied and was successful. I thought I'd cracked it.

My next fight was scheduled back at the Magna Centre in Rotherham against Jay Morris from the Isle of Wight. He was a tough kid and I had a horrible camp because of arguments between my sisters, Michelle and myself. My head was all over the place. I wasn't training or eating right.

Everything got interrupted because I was filming the show over in Argentina, three weeks before the contest. It would have been worth it if I'd won and picked up the ten grand prize money, but I didn't. I came second.

When I came back from the airport, Michelle and my sisters Chanelle and Nyeesha were waiting for me at Mum's house. I walked through the door and into the middle of massive row. There'd been a misunderstanding involving Michelle's son Summerby.

He claimed that Chanelle had spoken to him aggressively and hit him. She denied it and everything kicked off. It turned really nasty, spilled out into the street. I tried to intervene to keep the peace and Nyeesha punched me full in the face. What a homecoming! I was so shocked! To be fair it was a decent shot for a girl who'd never done any training.

I couldn't believe she'd done it. 'I am never speaking to you again,' I told her. There'd been troubles with my sisters ever since I got with Michelle. They never liked her. They thought she was using me to act as a father figure to her kids, but that was the first time it boiled over into physical confrontation. It caused a massive rift in my family.

I actually spoke to Dave and told him I wanted to pull out. My camp hadn't been good enough, I'd been away and my weight was all over the place, but Dave was insistent. He really wanted me to do this one. He refused to listen.

'This is your gateway fight,' he told me. 'It's too important to pull out of. After this one, big things are going to happen for you. You're going to be able to train full-time. I'm working on a sponsor.'

A few days before fight-night I was at home and Spencer Fearon, a London-based manager/promoter and associate of Dave's, phoned me up. I didn't know him, Dave must have given him my number. He's a real character, a great talker.

'Is this Jerome?' he said. 'Oh great, I'm really happy to be speaking with you. I saw your fight with Henry Janes. I was there. You did fantastic that night, such an exciting performance. I was so impressed. We could work together me and you. I've been speaking to Dave about you, I'm really interested in how you're developing.'

He told me about some of the stuff he was involved with in London and although he didn't say it in so many words it sounded like he was going to come in, get involved in my career. He'd said he'd speak to me again after the contest. I listened keenly, he had real charisma. What he was saying excited me, it could only be of benefit, I thought.

Although there was motivation in that conversation, in the run-up to the fight everything still felt messed up. There was an eight million pound lottery rollover that week and I was one number away from hitting that jackpot. I got five numbers and ended up with £1,500. I remember it so well because there were three lines I was using and I put my birthday number (24), on all of them. For some reason, on the last line I missed out the number 24. If I'd left it in, it would have given me the jackpot. It might sound silly, but it gave me a feeling that luck was against me.

Physically I wasn't right at all either. Morris was nearly 10st 12lb at the weigh-in and I came in at 10st 10lb, meaning it was a light middleweight bout, two divisions above my normal weight class. That suited him much more than me. He sometimes even boxed at middleweight. I was never even a proper welterweight, let alone light middle.

All that affected my psychology. The family problems only made matters worse. My confidence slipped. Morris didn't have a great record but he was no mug and everyone knew it. He'd beaten Curtis the year before. Dave got hold of me in the dressing room. He could tell I wasn't in the best frame of mind.

'Listen,' he said. 'You're a better boxer than Curtis. Just use your brain, move around and stick him. You've got this.'

Morris knew I'd been away for the TV stuff and he knew that I'd been getting some publicity after the Janes knockout, so he was bang up for it. He had a chance to steal a bit of my thunder. In the end it was a scrappy affair but I thought I landed the cleaner work.

He hurt me with a low blow in the third, but the ref ignored it, so he did it again. There were a couple of headbutts as well.

In the corner before the fourth Dave sounded anxious.

'Come on, don't let the fight slip away from you. Stay busy, outwork him.'

It was easier said than done. He old manned me, Morris, roughed me up. The last two rounds were tight. I still thought I beat him but the ref, Michael Alexander didn't. He gave it to Morris by a point. I had never felt so deflated.

Afterwards Dave was despondent too. He shook his head and looked down at the floor.

'You don't realise what you've lost here,' he said.

I didn't know what to think about that. I've often wondered what was going on and he never did tell me what that was all about. Losing a scrappy fight against a tough kid by one point shouldn't seem like a big deal. It shouldn't, but it did.

My mate and training partner Navid Mansouri was on after me. He told me later that before he started warming up on the pads he asked Dave how I was.

'Fuck Jerome,' Dave told him. 'It's all about you now.'

I was shocked when Nav told me, but in a way I wasn't surprised. Nav only got a draw himself that night. It wasn't a good show for our gym.

Needless to say, I never heard about sponsors or anything. Fearon didn't call me back. From that point in time, from when I got that first defeat, as far as the business of boxing was concerned, I was lost.

I was never given the opportunity for a rematch, like Curtis. After Curtis lost to Morris, he boxed him again for a title, only an International Masters title, but a title nonetheless. Curtis got the win and picked up his first belt. When I asked Dave for a rematch he would shake his head.

'He doesn't want a rematch,' he'd say. 'We can't really afford it, it wouldn't work out for us financially.'

I was a non-ticket seller and now my '0' had gone too. I'd look at my record on BoxRec and see that red 'L' next to my fifth fight. All the buzz from the Janes KO had disappeared.

Dave hummed and hawed about when I could box again and it turned into another long delay. Five months passed between the Morris loss and me re-entering the ring in Birmingham against a guy called Daniel Micalleff. It was a strange one.

Micallef was Maltese and had won two fights over there, but the British Boxing Board of Control didn't recognise his bouts as legitimate, so officially he was a debutant. Dave was promoting the show and I was in the home corner, but I didn't have to sell tickets. It took the pressure off but it was like I was there to make up the numbers, really. The fight was made at welter but the atmosphere between me and Dave was wrong. Maybe I was too sensitive. I lost motivation and trained and ate badly again. There were no external excuses this time. It was my fault. Perhaps I should have been tougher mentally.

I came in two pounds overweight, so I didn't even make welterweight. Dave was not happy and fined me £50 out of my purse.

'You should knock this boy out,' he told me. 'If you hit him with the power we know you've got, you can take him out.'

Once we got in there, Micallef threw a lot of shots and he could dig a bit, but technically he wasn't in my league. I did what I needed to do but held back from committing myself. Why should I? If you can win without taking shots, that's what the science of boxing is all about. He hardly laid a glove on me. I out-boxed him and won every round.

I was quite pleased. After the fight Dave said to me, 'well done on the win, but I have to tell you Jerome, the public want entertainment. They want battles, lots of punches landed. They want action. You can't keep moving around and pot-shotting.'

He drew a sharp breath and fixed me in the eye.

'You're not selling tickets and your fights are boring.'

The Beginning
Of The End

TWO months later Dave put me back on one of his Rotherham shows against a Kenyan welterweight called Geoffrey Munika. Munika had knocked out former English champion Ryan Barrett and had scored a draw against British champ and world title challenger Lee Purdy. The idea was to test me by putting me in with someone who could stretch me a bit, but because no one had heard of Munika and I still had the loss to Morris hanging over my head, ticket selling was harder than ever.

I shifted just under 40 for that fight. Dave called me into the office at the venue. He made himself crystal clear.

'You need to do better than this,' he said. 'It's as simple as that. You're not pulling your weight with these sort of sales. You're lucky I'm still putting you on.'

It made me feel guilty. Although I understood why, it bothered me that some lads could sell tickets and I couldn't. It played on my mind. When we'd had these sorts of conversations in my early career I'd always said that things would pick up and I'd gather momentum later, but the opposite was happening. I was selling fewer tickets as time went by, not more.

Munika turned out to be the most awkward guy I ever fought. He chucked shots from weird angles and threw me off stride. I got caught a few too many times for my liking and overall I was disappointed with my performance. I felt very flat, but still did enough to win. It took my record to 6–1.

Things felt like they were slowly grinding to a halt though. Dave was fed up because I wasn't making him any money.

Other fighters were leaving him and there was often a weird, muted atmosphere in the gym. I was tense most of the time, because I felt like my career was stagnating. We had a few little arguments.

One time Dave accused me of being arrogant and said he had had overheard me being dismissive of his ticket concerns. I really didn't think I'd said what he accused me of. I began to have serious doubts if boxing was going to work for me.

It was seven months before I fought again and my next contest did nothing to change things. I boxed the journeyman Sid Razak at light middle. Razak didn't come to win and I took every round in a nothing fight. The hall was silent throughout. For that one I set a new personal low of 15 ticket sales.

'Do you know how much money I'm losing?' It was becoming Dave's most familiar question. There wasn't much I could say.

Razak had a record of 8–90. All respect to him, he performs a certain role in the business, but it was difficult to get myself up for the contest. He was a similar opponent to Johnny Greaves, just not as funny, the sort of guy you box on your debut, or in your first couple of bouts. All he was going to do was come in, stay on the back-foot and try not to get hurt. It was my eighth bout, but I felt I was going backwards.

After that one I tried to force the issue a bit. We had several discussions about where things were going. During one of our more heated conversations about ticket sales he said to me, 'You do realise I'm not your promoter, only your manager.'

I checked the small print on our contract and he was right. It didn't make much sense to me. I mainly boxed on his shows, in the home corner. I was trained and managed by him but technically he didn't promote me. Once I allowed that to sink in and had a think, it did explain a few things. I didn't feel he had really made the effort to get my name out there and publicise me. My name was rarely in the papers, but his big ticket sellers were always getting coverage.

He used to say to me, 'Keep at it. If you want to achieve in this game and win titles, you've got to work really hard in all ways.' I tried to, I kept myself training, I put everything into my fights, but it just wasn't working for me. I found motivating myself for such small reward so difficult. I still loved boxing, but it was slowly breaking my heart.

After the Razak fight it wasn't clear when or if Dave would get me another contest. I stayed around the gym whenever possible and continued sparring.

The Beginning Of The End

As time had gone by a few of Dave's fighters had dwindled away. Even Curtis had left to train with Jon Pegg in Birmingham. I wondered why, but still tried to convince myself that it was the best place for me to be.

It's so important for a boxer to have backers who believe in them, but I felt Dave had stopped believing in me because I couldn't sell tickets. It seems strange though, when I look back over my time with Dave. Although there were problems, he also did so much good for me. I find it hard to decide what I think of him.

The time after the Razak fight ended up being an 18-month break from the ring. It was almost a retirement. I felt directionless and Dave gave me a job working with the youngsters at Coldwell Boxing. His partner, Spencer Fearn ran a national service called Life Skills and we became one of his sub-providers. It was probably the most rewarding job I ever had but I had to make sacrifices in order to do it, the main one being limiting my boxing training to work full-time.

That hadn't been my intention at the beginning. I thought I could box around the job. When Dave suggested it he had said we could train before work, me and Nav and a couple of others who were still with him. That didn't end up happening. In fact I hardly trained with Dave ever again after the Razak fight. He had lost interest and the bits I did were on my own.

The joy had all gone out of it for him, I think. You could tell he didn't want to do it anymore. He kept saying to me, 'It's business, boxing's a business,' and to tell the truth I hated hearing it. It was sucking the joy out of it for me as well.

I did enjoy the work though. It felt like I was giving something back to the community. We were working with hard-to-reach teenagers and young adults. No ' vas ever the same. Most of them had issues with authority, some had learning difficulties, some were very bright, many were angry. They carried their pasts and traumas with them, like bags. It was our job to take those bags away, or at least make them lighter. All were treated equally. They came to us for boxing training, sports education, English and Information Technology lessons.

The boxing really helped to instil discipline and respect, building confidence and self-esteem. We saw differences very quickly. I really believed in what we were doing but it was the first classroom teaching job I ever had. Originally I was only drafted in to coach boxing and run the fitness classes, but as more students were referred a need arose for another tutor in the classroom. I was a bit dubious as I'd not done anything like it before but as the subjects being taught were similar to the qualifications I gained at college, I felt comfortable teaching them.

There was one lad in particular, by the name of Tom, whose story was so typical of a lot of the youngsters we had there. When he was 14, he fell in with the wrong crowd and became an alcoholic, drinking three litres of cider a day as well as taking drugs. He was disenchanted with school and slipping into street culture. His prospects did not look promising at all.

Tom began as a student for a few months then became an apprentice after gaining some qualifications with us. I helped him realise that to get where he wanted to be, he needed to move himself away from the people who had a negative impact on him. I told him that it's all about mindset and positive thinking. If your mind is in the right place there isn't much that can go wrong. He needed a balanced training routine and a healthy lifestyle to keep him on the right path and we gave him that. It thrilled me to see how well he did.

As ever though, boxing was still on my mind. It may have been a while since I had been in the ring, but I still saw myself as a fighter. After I had finished working with Tom one afternoon, Dave called me into his office. He knew I was keen to get fighting again and wanted to discuss it.

He was all smiles to begin with.

'How would you like to see it going from here?' he asked.

I told him I'd like to pick up from where I left off. I only had the one defeat and seven wins. It was still a good record. Maybe I could aim for the Central Area title as a starting point? Then build things up from there. He made a little face, his tone changed.

'Look Jerome,' he said. 'Let's get real. You're not getting any younger, are you? You're 28, you've never sold many tickets and the fact is its going to be very difficult to push you along for titles. You'd make far more money boxing on the road. You could fight regularly and get decent money. There's a living in it. You know I'd rather see my fighters pay off their mortgage than end their career with nothing.'

I hadn't been expecting that.

'I hear what you're saying Dave,' I replied. 'But I'm not really bothered about the money. Of course having it would be nice, but so long as I can get in the ring and give it my all then I'm happy. I want to try and do something.'

'But your age, mate,' he said again.

Back in the 1960s and 70s, 28 *was* old for someone in my weight division, but not in the 21st century. The best welterweight in the world, Floyd Mayweather, was 36 at the time. The British light welter champion Darren Hamilton was 34. I still felt I had plenty of time.

'Come on, look at Darren Hamilton,' I protested. 'He's British champion.'

Dave just flipped. There must have been something bubbling under the surface that I hadn't been aware of. He jumped up from his chair and slammed his hands on the desk.

'You're delusional Jerome! You're delusional,' he shouted. 'Hamilton lives in the gym, how on Earth can you compare yourself to him? You're fucking delusional! He does much more then you, he lives and breathes boxing. Get real!'

In that moment he looked possessed, like some kind of maniac. I sat back, shocked. There had been times before when I had wondered, but Dave had just made it clear how little belief he really had in me. I looked back at him in silence.

'He picks his fights well,' I thought. He's only gone off at me like that because he knows I'm not the sort of the guy who'd lose their temper and chin him. Many other fighters would have.

The Beginning Of The End

For a moment hatred welled up inside. Here was a man who only stood 5ft 3in, who claimed to have got into boxing after being bullied as a kid, becoming the bully. What a great use of power to try to crush any confidence I had, to try to force me down a path I didn't want to take.

I felt a rush of sadness. Where was that happy, inspirational Dave who got me into boxing as a kid? The one who used to take me to nightclubs and ask me to look after his dog? He had disappeared. Instead there was this human chameleon, who changed his attitudes, opinions and feelings to suit different situations. A businessman, looking only at the world as one big balance sheet. To cap it all off, I had just signed a new three year contract with him. Why couldn't he have started this conversation before?

I thought about it all for a while after that meeting, but there was no sense in it, to my eyes. The only conclusion I could draw was that Dave was feeling the pinch after his big name fighters had left and he wanted to start making money off me himself. By putting me in as an opponent on other people's shows, it would guarantee him some sort of income.

We avoided each other at work after that and I saw very little of him. I just threw myself back into grafting with the youngsters, which took my mind off my boxing problems. The job did help me to grow as a person, despite the lull in my boxing career. I witnessed the effect we had the students and it made me feel good.

Yes, I helped people get fit, stay motivated and perform exercises correctly and safely, but it was more

181

about growth, for them and me. We all need to grow. When you stop growing, you start dying.

I started to get really into it and think perhaps it was the sort of thing I could do for a while, but the job only lasted a year in the end. There was a cut in funding and like most other employees, I was made redundant. It was disappointing.

I was at the gym shortly after that on my own, keeping my fitness up. Dave called me over. His face was flat and expressionless.

'I'm giving up coaching,' he said. 'I'm moving on to concentrate on other things, so you'll have to find yourself a new trainer.'

By that stage I hadn't boxed for over a year. Dave hadn't really trained me for months anyway but myself and Nav had been with him a long time. We were both pretty upset really. The morale in the camp had been terrible but I'd been determined not to give up and stick it out. I convinced myself everything would come good in the end. Now it all felt like a massive waste of time.

The thought of retirement crossed my mind, again. All the difficulties of sustaining a boxing career were tiring me out, but I deep down I knew I'd regret it. My prime years were still ahead of me. If I walked away, I'd always wonder, 'What if?'

I had a conversation with Nav. We both had our suspicions.

What had it all been about? Why had he kept us on the backburner for so long? Were we just there just to create an atmosphere in the gym and help with sparring? High quality sparring can be expensive when you have to pay for it. Maybe that's how we earned our places?

It seemed like we had just been supporting actors in the film. Then when Curtis left him and Ryan retired, Dave fell out of love with it all because his stars had disappeared. I felt used.

I thought it over for a couple of days and spoke to Michelle, but in the end there was only one decision to make. I still wanted to box. I had to.

I thought of Chris Smedley and how maybe I should have stayed with him from the beginning. It didn't feel right to go and approach him again now. At the time Nav was English champ and already had contacts to go and train with Oliver Harrison. I had no one.

I heard that Ryan Rhodes was training fighters, so I asked him. He said he wasn't going to have any time for it at the moment. A few people said to go to the Ingle camp, but I was hesitant. I had heard mixed things about training there, so for a while I just trained myself with a few of the keep fitters at Dave's gym.

That didn't really work, not if I wanted to continue fighting professionally. My motivation diminished. I needed a trainer. You need someone watching your every move, criticising and analysing.

Nav suggested hooking up with one of his old coaches, Ian Baines, at the Millennium boxing gym in Rotherham, around the corner from where I was working. There were lots of fighters there to spar, it was a decent gym and Bainsey was a good bloke by all accounts.

I went down and spoke to him. He was a cool guy, relaxed and funny, but also honest. We decided to give it a go.

He just wanted to take a look at me at first and let me do my thing, to see what I was like. I thought I'd be clever and do something wrong to see if he picked it up. I'd drop my hands after throwing or leave my feet in the wrong place. He always spotted it.

I started training with Ian in June 2013 and things developed quickly. We talked about career progression. Despite having nothing to do with my training, Dave was still my manager and his words remained in the back of my head.

'The crowd want entertainment…Your fights are boring.'

In training with Bainsey we emphasised throwing more punches and getting fitter – higher intensity, fan-friendly fighting.

We began speaking about the possibility of me getting in the ring again in the near future. Dave lined me up with a guy called Michael Mooney, from Worcester. The fight was set for the Ponds Forge arena in Sheffield on 4 October. Mooney was a good fighter, although he boxed mainly in the away corner and had a mixed record.

It would be a tough, competitive contest for my first bout back.

Bainesy got me really motivated and I trained like a demon. I actually enjoyed it again. I wanted to make a statement and make the second act of my career a success. I desperately wanted to prove Dave wrong. Soon I was in my best shape ever.

The Beginning Of The End

By then Ryan had started training a few fighters at Dave's gym. He had a good little stable including Ross Burkinshaw, David Fiddler, Lee Appleyard, Jamie Robinson and Zack Collins. He was on the lookout for good sparring for his lads. He got in touch. Bainsey and I welcomed the chance.

We went down there and Dave was sitting by the ring, watching the session, which made for an interesting atmosphere. I was on fire. I had my iPhone connected to the music system pumping out my beats and I was untouchable. I sparred with Ross, Zack, Lee, and finished with Jamie.

As each three-minute round went by I stayed in the ring waiting to take on the next person, whoever it was. I did what I pleased and felt so relaxed and comfortable. No one laid a glove on me, while I picked off the other lads at will.

Someone whispered to turn off the music. They thought it might help to throw me off my stride. There were those who thought I was a fair-weather fighter and only boxed well when things were going my way; that I couldn't dig in when I needed to. People had said those kinds of things since the Morris fight.

The trick didn't work and I just boxed even better. Music, no music, it made no difference. As the final round finished I smiled inside. I had performed so well.

Afterwards all the guys were raving about the way I boxed, saying they couldn't wait to see me fight. Ryan told me how impressed he was, after such a long lay-off and how much I had come on. Even Dave made positive comments, saying that my workrate had improved and that if I boxed like that, people would enjoy watching me. I was so happy. It felt good to be back.

Then two days before the Mooney fight, Dave sent me a text message. I knew what it would say before I opened it.

'Afternoon!' it said. 'I need to know how many tickets you've done please. Got to let the venue know for set up.'

I replied that I had sold 42, but was hoping to shift a few more before the night. He didn't comment. The following day, 24 hours before I was due in the ring, he sent me another.

'What are you on now?'

'45' I replied. 'Still a few more people to get cash off.'

This time he texted back straight away.

'It's your choice whether you box or not but you know the deal mate. I need to let the opponent know ASAP if the fight is off. As it is you're on about £250.'

I didn't want to scratch out. Physically I was on top form, but it was obvious that Dave was having second thoughts.

Mooney and I both weighed in on the night, inside the light welter limit. I was buzzing for it, probably more excited for a fight than I had been since boxing Janes on the world title undercard.

I didn't even think about the money. I was back in Sheffield, fighting in my correct weight class and ready to put on a show.

I began my psychological preparations, talking to myself, getting psyched up. Then two hours before fight time, Damien Harry, one of the directors of Coldwell Boxing, came into the dressing room.

'Jerome! Dave needs to see you in his office now,' he said.

I knew from the tone of his voice that something was up. Warily, I followed him out. As I followed him down there I saw Maxi Hughes, another of Dave's fighters, pacing back and forth in the corridor.

Dave looked really glum when I opened the door. He was sitting behind his desk, eyes down, as if he had a dead puppy on his lap.

'This is one of the last things I would want to do,' he said, raising his face to look at me. 'It's devastating. I'm really sorry Jerome. I'd never want to do this to you, but Maxi's opponent has pulled out with an injury. His manager says he's been stung by a fucking insect. Weirdest excuse I've ever heard. We tried to bring a replacement in, but he's pulled out as well. So the way it's looking, we've got no alternative but to give your opponent to Maxi. What do you think about that mate?'

I didn't know what to say. I wanted to scream. All fired up, in perfect shape, just to get slapped in the face.

'What do you reckon I think about that?' I asked.

'I'm sorry Jerome, there's no other way,' he said.

I knew what was going on. Maxi sold more tickets than me. At only 23 he was younger than me too and they thought he had better earning potential for the future. They were looking after their investment. I could understand that, on one level, but it showed how little my career was valued. I protested a little, but there was nothing I could do.

Dave obviously felt bad about it. He gave me £500 and refunded the ticket money of my supporters, but that couldn't change the way I felt. It wasn't about a bit of cash, it was about the wasted months of training and my future as a fighter. Dave was my manager. He was in control of my career, but he wasn't even trying to move it upwards. If anything he was dragging it down.

I left the office, walked down the corridor and punched the wall. I had to punch something. Gearing up for a fight that doesn't happen is like being teased all night by a sexy girl, who strips, tells you to do the same then gets her things and leaves. You build so much energy but then have no release.

I had to go outside for air before going in to the arena to face my ticket-buyers. Some of my friends and family were livid. I broke the news to them as they arrived to take their seats. One or two wanted to find Dave and have it out with him. I had to placate them. It wasn't easy. I was so angry myself.

When I went back into the changing room, the other home boxers seemed to know what had happened. It went quiet. Chad Gaynor was in there, Nav, obviously Maxi Hughes. They all looked at the floor, no one wanted to meet my eye, as if my lowly status could somehow be contagious. I had reached another low point on my boxing journey.

Maybe I should have made more of a fuss. I often think that. I should have been forceful, pushed harder for what I wanted. But I didn't know many people in the business. I told myself that in Sheffield, Dave was the best man for the job. No one had his contacts and know-how.

Fan-Friendly Fighting

A FEW days later Dave said he'd get me on another show in Manchester to soften the blow, but that didn't end up happening. The next best option he had was an event he was doing at Ice Sheffield, in December 2013, two months after I should have fought Mooney. I accepted it wearily. I wanted to fight, but things were really getting me down.

I got back into training for a couple of weeks then Dave said he'd lined up a guy called Mark McKray, a Jamaican journeyman from London, as my opponent. What made that interesting was that McKray was the guy who'd pulled out of fighting Maxi Hughes at Ponds Forge. He'd obviously recovered from his insect bites and was looking for work again.

The contest would be at light-welter and once I knew it would be McKray in the other corner I began to really look forward to the bout. In a way I blamed him for what had happened before. My training became more vigorous. I had vindictive intentions. I was going to make him pay. I told Dave, 'I'm gonna knock that fucker out. He's gonna get it. I'm still fuming about last time.'

For three weeks I trained like a madman with Bainsey. He was really pleased with how I'd regained my motivation after all the disappointment. My fitness levels came back quickly and I felt sharp in sparring.

Then on 4 December, eight days before the fight, I got a message from Dave.

'Just so you know – McKray not looking good now, looking elsewhere.'

This is the sort of thing that people outside of the business don't see or understand. You focus on a particular fight, a particular opponent for a reason, then it all gets changed. You're constantly having the rug pulled from under your feet. This one wasn't Dave's fault though. McKray had boxed in Swansea at the end of November and got bashed up a bit. There was no chance he'd be ready to fight me on the 13th.

I tried to keep my spirits up and stayed in the gym with no idea who I'd be fighting or if I still had a fight at all. Ian worked more and more on bringing my aggressive side out. Increasing my punch output, keeping my guard up higher. In my early days I had kept my left hand low and used it to gauge the distance. Ian stopped me doing that.

It was the last chance for my career to take off. I would need to sacrifice my defensive instincts to provide more entertainment. Get people talking about me, create a buzz, it's what Dave had always wanted. And I thought it was what I needed to do.

Four days before the show, Dave got in touch to say he'd found a Scottish guy called Billy Campbell, but if I took it I'd have to box a four-rounder with him at welter. He wouldn't be able to come in lighter than 10st 6lb. Campbell was 3–3 at the time and had done some mixed martial arts (MMA) as well as boxing. He was a tough guy, a real fighting man and that was pretty much all I knew, but I didn't feel I had a choice. By then it was a year and a half since my last fight and if I turned this one down, who knew when my next opportunity would come?

On the night the extra weight made me feel heavy and sluggish. I guess it's what they call ring rust, but I performed decently enough. We were first fight on and the venue was quite empty. It was a good contest. He was very strong.

I tried to come out quickly and use my newly developed aggression. We had several hectic exchanges but I always felt I came out better. By the third I was dominating. His left eye swelled up.

In the last I went after him. I didn't want anyone saying this fight was boring. I rocked him with a big hook in the centre of the ring and chased him down. We were giving and taking, I had him going, then out of nowhere he caught me with a huge right. It wobbled me. I staggered back on shaky legs. He got me again. I was in trouble. The noise of the crowd increased. Everything went out of focus.

Luckily we were inside the last 20 seconds or God knows where I'd have ended up. I didn't have to weather the storm for long. I just bit down on my gum shield and had it out with him. My knees were dipping but I hung in there and made it to final bell. The small crowd in the arena went mad. The commentators on internet TV were effusive, saying what a great contest it had been.

Barnesy was pleased with my performance but concerned with how I'd left myself open at the end.

'You're staying in the pocket too long after you throw,' he said. 'You need to unload then take a half-step back, then move back into range when you're ready. It's good that you're throwing more shots but you don't want to get into wars.'

Dave made a joke about the last round but he was pleased too. 'You're giving the crowd what they want,' he said. 'It's so much better!'

I was just happy I'd stayed on my feet and got the 'W'. Did the new style suit me? At the time it wasn't a question I asked. It suited everyone else and I just wanted to get my career moving again.

On the 16th, three days after the Campbell fight, I was driving home after working at the gym and Dave phoned me. He never phoned me at that sort of time, so I thought it had to be important. I pulled over by the side of the road and took the call.

'Something's come up,' he said. 'Frankie Gavin's people have been in touch. He's down to fight in Leeds next week and his opponent has pulled out. They're looking for a stand-in and I thought of you. I know its short notice but it's a huge opportunity, plus they're offering £10,000 for ten rounds.'

It was a lot of money and in some ways the sort of chance you dream of. At the time Gavin was British and Commonwealth champion. As an amateur he'd been ranked number one in the world. He was a big name. If I could go in and beat him it would put me on the map.

For those reasons I was tempted, but there were a few issues. Firstly Gavin was a welterweight, albeit a small one. It's one thing to take a fight with the first really top-drawer boxer you've faced, but to step up a weight division to do it is a tall order. Gavin had previously knocked out Denton Vassell, who I'd sparred and found very strong.

As well as giving away size, I'd be going in as the away fighter on his promoter's show, meaning I'd be highly unlikely to get a points decision if it went the distance. Plus I'd only just come through a tough fight in which I'd been badly wobbled. Campbell's fourth-round barrage had concussed me a bit. It had taken me a couple of days to shake off the effects and I hadn't been training due to shooting pains in my head. The Gavin fight would come just two weeks after that one. I thanked Dave but told him I'd have to think about it.

'I'm gonna need an answer off you quickly,' he said.

I put the phone down and called Bainsey straight away. He confirmed what I felt – it was too soon after the Campbell fight, I wouldn't be ready for a ten-rounder and I'd just be offering myself up as a sacrificial lamb. Getting up in front a big audience and getting taken apart wouldn't be good for career or health.

I called Dave back and told him I couldn't take the fight, that I'd spoken with my trainer and we'd both agreed it wouldn't be in my best interests. We intended to wait for the after-effects of the Campbell bout to wear off, then get back into full training. We reckoned I'd be ready to box again by February.

Dave was bitterly disappointed.

'Think of the money,' he said.

Money for who? I thought. Was Dave looking forward to his percentage?

'I'm not about the money, Dave.'

'It's not just money, though is it? This is massive. You will probably never get another opportunity like this.'

'Look if everything was okay I would take the fight in a heartbeat. But I'd want a proper training camp to fight Gavin. The timing's wrong and I'm still feeling the last one. The money would be great but I don't want to get up there and look like a punk for anyone.'

'I'm sure you'd be okay,' Dave said. 'Think of what this could do for you.'

'Sorry Dave. It's a no.'

Not long after I got another call from Bainsey. He said that after speaking to me, Dave had phoned him asking why I turned down the fight. Dave badgered him, trying to convince him to speak to me again and tell me it would be okay. Ian said it was strange, that Dave was quite insistent and really wanted me to fight Gavin.

'You've done the right thing,' Bainsey said, 'I don't want to be looking your family in the eye in the hospital if anything went wrong, knowing that I'd took you to the ring when there was a problem.'

A day or so later Dave must have even got on to Curtis about the whole thing. Curtis had already fought Gavin, losing on a split decision in 2011. He phoned me, asking why I hadn't taken the fight, saying that Dave had been talking about it a lot. I explained what was wrong and Curtis understood where I was coming from.

'You've got to do what's best for you,' he told me. 'You are the one going into that ring so you have to be right for it.'

It felt like I was being set up as cannon fodder. What bothered me was that Dave was the one doing the setting. With that sort of preparation, I wouldn't have had a chance against a good welterweight champion who had done three months training. Surely that was obvious?

So why had Dave been so keen for me to take it? Was he determined to turn me into a paid loser? Gavin was an elite pro and it felt like Coldwell was happy to throw me to the lions.

Fifteen Minutes Of Fame

Smith – Now to a small hall fight in May. Sheffield's Jerome 'Wipeout' Wilson and Cameroon's Yorkshire-based Serge Ambomo, well they went to war for six rounds. Up and down, up and down. Ambomo eventually took the decision. Johnny, you were there weren't you?

Nelson – I popped in and they were going crazy! Joe, you must like this kind of thing? Up and downers, a bit of excitement?

Calzaghe – Well I didn't like being involved in them sort of things…

[Awkward laughter]

Calzaghe – I'd prefer to be on the safe side of the ropes watching the fight, but yeah, obviously that's value for money. It's great when you get small-hall boys, going in like that in six rounders and it's probably fight of the night.

Nelson – The thing is there were two shows on in Sheffield that night and both shows got the crowds going. It's good for the paying public. They had action all the way through

Smith – Whatever level, 50–50 or 55–45, even-stevens matches is what the public demand and they're getting many more of these days.

Woodhall – That's what everyone wants to see, you know, two kids having a real go at it. Donkey derby springs to mind, no disrespect to them, great fight, great entertainment.

Smith – Absolutely, from a hard-core trade show.

Sky presenter Adam Smith and former world champions Johnny Nelson, Joe Calzaghe and Richie Woodhall discussing the first Wilson v Ambomo fight on Ringside *on Sky Sports.*

* * * * *

I was expecting more from my career, I guess. I had assumed that one day, somehow, the early promise and all the great gym sessions and spars would translate into something concrete, that eventually it would all come together and I would have my time at the top. It never happened.

After turning down the Gavin fight I didn't hear much from Dave for a while. I still saw him occasionally and we'd exchange a few words of banter, but as a manager I'd developed such serious reservations about him. He'd begun to have discussions about a kind of partnership with Eddie Hearn of Matchroom Sport, the country's biggest promoter.

Up to that time Dave's shows had been streamed on the internet on the Coldwell TV app. Hearn wanted to bring a number of medium-sized promoters, like Dave under his umbrella and show them on a new service called Matchroom Fight Pass. As Matchroom already had the Sky TV deal, this was exciting news for boxers looking for opportunities. A good performance on Fight Pass could see future fights end up on Sky. TV is always where the real recognition and money comes in.

Tentative offers for fights came my way. A bout against unbeaten Welshman Chris Jenkins in Cardiff in early February was mentioned. I turned it down as I had been ill. There were possibilities of boxing Jack Catterall in Manchester and a kid called Hugh Grey in Scotland. All three were away corner jobs. None of them ended up happening, but it seemed that Dave had made the decision for me about how my career should go.

I told him I'd be interested in entering a Prizefighter tournament, where boxers compete over three round contests, with quarter-finals, semis and final all on the same night. Matchroom and Sky were doing a light welterweight edition and my name had been bandied around online.

'I already asked Eddie for you,' Dave said. 'But he only wants ticket sellers or names.'

'But my name's on the internet?'

'Eddie does that all the time. There's about 30 names put out for it. He's just testing the water. Popular fighters equal ticket sales and viewing figures. Sorry mate.'

The next name to get put my way was former European champion Lenny Daws. He was recouping after losing his title to an Italian in suspicious circumstances, when his opponent appeared to have an illegal substance applied to a cut. Again it was an away corner offer, on a James DeGale undercard in Kent. Again I knocked it back.

I wanted to fight but the thought of going on the road to do it worried me. That's how guys like Johnny Greaves and Sid Razak made a living, boxing away, losing every week. Dave used to say that if you're good enough you can still build a career in the away corner, but everyone knew the odds were hugely stacked against you.

Just when it looked like I was heading for another period of inactivity Dave offered me a contest against another Sheffield fighter called Sam 'The Sensation' O'Maison. He was an Ingle boxer and known as a bit of a puncher. People thought of him as a decent prospect and he was unbeaten in eight.

The contest would be on one of Dave's shows on 9 May at the Ice Arena. Although Dave was the show's promoter and also my manager, the offer was again to box as the away fighter. It seemed that's where I was heading and there was nothing I could do about it.

I had seen this sort of thing before, as Dave had managed and trained guys like Daniel Thorpe and Carl Baker who filled the journeyman role. They would fight on his promotions as the opponent, lose, take their money and go home. There's nothing wrong with that, but it wasn't the way I saw myself. I still had ambition. I didn't want to rack up a string of defeats.

Out of sheer desire to fight, I accepted the contest. Dave explained that although O'Maison was in the home corner he wouldn't sell enough to cover all costs. Rather than receive a wage I would be paid in tickets. In other words whatever I sold, I could keep, once I'd given Dave his 15 per cent manager's cut and ten per cent training fees for Bainsey. It was a shit deal, but I still took it. It would be my tenth pro fight, in my home city and it was unlikely I would make more than pocket change.

I went back to work with Bainsey and tried to put all of that stuff behind me. Ian's a good man and he believed in me. 'You'll beat O'Maison no problem,' he said. 'You're streets ahead of him.' I used that for motivation.

'It's not about money,' I would say to myself. 'It's about proving what I can do and making Ian proud.'

I was very confident. O'Maison liked to move a bit, like me, but was small at the weight and I knew I had his number. I couldn't wait.

Predictably, the fight fell through. O'Maison boxed a guy called Jan Balog live on Channel 5 six weeks before our contest was scheduled. He won, but broke his hand. I waited for Dave to come back to me with news.

At first I was frustrated, but two days later he told me that the Ingles were considering putting Junior 'The Hitter' Witter on in O'Maison's place. The idea excited me straight away. Witter was 40 years old but had been a world champion at light welter for a couple of years. Later he had won the British welterweight title, before losing it to Frankie Gavin in 2012.

Despite his age, he was a big name. I had sparred him before and knew I could take him. Even though it was at welter, with a proper training camp behind me, I knew. It could be the opportunity I needed to catapult myself into the rankings and the spotlight.

Dave offered me an extra £500 on top of the tickets to take the Witter fight and I accepted gladly. It was another all Sheffield match-up, but one with much more cachet than fighting O'Maison. On 28 March I received the official confirmation that the fight had been made.

'It's another big opportunity,' Dave said. 'Witter is ranked fifth in Britain so if you beat him you can gatecrash the top ten. Remember his age. If you're ever going to make a statement its now. Keep him off balance with a double jab. Don't throw single shots at him. Get some good sparring, go spar Frankie or some members of the GB squad. Don't fuck about with familiarity.'

It was the first piece of boxing advice he had given me in ages.

A week later, Witter pulled out of the fight. The official reason was that he had been moving some stuff in a house and a radiator had dropped on his head. You really couldn't make this stuff up. Coincidentally, at the time I was doing a personal training qualification at college and he was on the course too. I saw him there and he was fine. The consensus was he had just decided he didn't fancy it anymore. Dave was as annoyed as I was.

'He's too old and you're too young and fast. He's realised that. There's too much to lose for him.'

In the end Witter contested another bout eight days after we were supposed to fight, so whatever injury he had can't have been that bad. Once again I found myself in a complete mess.

I had been booked in as the away fighter for the show on 9 May against two ticket sellers who had taken the fight and then withdrawn. I had already sold about 30 tickets myself and was very keen to stay on the bill, but without a home boxer to go in with I was screwed.

A last minute offer to box Sam 'The Savage' Eggington came up (at the time he was just a good prospect, now he's Commonwealth welterweight champion). It was at two days' notice and offered at light middleweight, so I turned it down.

'Can't you find me an opponent at light welter?' I pleaded with Dave. 'I really want to fight.'

I tried frantically to come up with solutions to stay on the 9 May show, figuring out how many tickets I would have to sell to pay for an opponent myself so there was no risk for Dave, suggesting all sorts of possibilities. I assured him I was doing everything I could to sell as many as possible this time.

Around then I had became a fully qualified fitness instructor and took up a position with a company called Prime Mover. Their clients were quite affluent, solicitors, business consultants, people like that. I enjoyed working with them. A lot of them were interested in me and what I was doing. Some offered support.

Several of them ran their own businesses and as my relationships with them built, they offered me sponsorships. For the first time since turning pro I had people willing to invest in my career, although they hadn't come through my manager, I had found them myself. It did make me stop and think, 'What am I paying Dave for?' Since the Morris loss I didn't feel he had done very much for me at all. I was battling away to make it work on my own.

My change of job meant that I hardly saw him at all, weakening our bond further. Despite that he reluctantly agreed to shift me to the home corner and look for someone to fight me. On 20 April I told him I had sold enough tickets to pay for an opponent and asked for an exact price so I could think about earning some money for myself.

'I thought your tickets were flying out and you had loads coming to watch you?' he asked. The question felt a little barbed. 'How many have you sold so far?'

'I've sold £1,730 worth so far. I'll do more when people get paid.'

'How many tickets is that?'

'Fourteen ringside and 25 standard.'

'Hope you move some more mate.'

On 28 April, a week and a half before the show, Dave texted me a name, 'Serge Ambomo'.

'Is that the guy who trained with you?' I asked.

'I didn't train him. He worked here for about a month before going to Glyn's. Cameroon asylum seeker. It'll be 10st 3lb the day before.'

Light welter was supposed to be 10st, but it was close enough. I accepted.

'Is he gonna make 10st 3lb though? He's flipping massive!'

'He's not as big as you, just has a bigger skull!'

'Okay, is he any good? I've not seen much of him?'

'He's decent but not a world beater. Was in the Olympics, strong but short. Won his first two.'

'Okay, I'll expect him to come and try to take my head off then.'

Dave came back to me later and said he'd agreed a purse of £1,600 for Serge. It was about £500 more than the standard away corner fee. Both camps saw it as a risky fight and Ambomo was no journeyman.

'Wow,' I told him, 'I'll be lucky if I've got enough left over for a pair of trainers.'

Realistically I was only looking at £200 to £300 for myself. Dave surprised me and offered to waive his percentage for the bout, a really nice gesture, which I appreciated. I just hoped that this one wouldn't fall through as well.

I started focusing my training on making weight. I'd need to be four pounds lighter on fight night than I would have been to box Witter. The sweatsuit came out of the cupboard, I cut down on my food intake and upped my fluids.

I looked Serge up on the internet and found a video of his last contest against Adam Salman, a welterweight from London. Salman's a tidy enough boxer, quite straight forward and strong. He had the better of Ambomo for the first three rounds. Serge just stood in front of him, swinging hooks, really. He appeared powerful, but one-dimensional, always looking for the big right hand.

In the fourth it all changed. Ambomo came out like a man possessed, trapped Salman on the ropes and landed a thunderous left hook. Salman staggered backwards and Serge followed, tearing into him with a fierce two-fisted assault. It was like watching a tiger pounce on a deer. Salman ended up doubled over in a neutral corner, with Ambomo landing shot after shot, until the referee came to his rescue. It was a brutal finish.

I watched the recording of Serge celebrating the win, with his Mohawk hairdo, hands raised, the boos of the hometown crowd reverberating around the York Hall. He lapped up the hatred. Here was a guy who had gone on the road and won, as Dave had been suggesting I could do. I felt he was lucky though. Sure, he'd looked powerful, even up at welter, but he was losing the fight clearly before the finish.

To fight me, he'd have to come in several pounds lighter, which would weaken him. I was a far better boxer than Salman too. I knew that. Quicker, better feet, more elusive. I was positive I could box this guy's ears off.

In the end I weighed in a pound and a half under, at 10st 1½lb. Ambomo was heavy. 10st 5lb. He would put weight on before the fight too, making it likely that by the time we fought he'd be much heavier than me. I had the option to make a fuss about it, but didn't. If he had been unable to go and shed the weight in a couple of hours it would have jeopardised the fight taking place. I'd been through enough crap with cancellations and changes.

Once we got in there, on the night, our styles just clashed. It's a funny thing that. It's like a chemistry experiment. Sometimes the physiques and techniques of two particular fighters combine in a way that produces dynamite. It was like that with me and Serge.

The first round I came out, boxing sharp, landed a few stiff jabs, was feeling the distance, having a look at him, then I threw the straight right, it caught him clean and – bang – he went down.

He got up and the ref gave him an eight count. I rushed out of my neutral corner, threw a couple of combos, punches in bunches and he touched down again. He bounced straight back up and amazingly the ref didn't give it. I went back to my boxing and won the round well, but that first should have been 10–7 for me.

Despite the bizarre officiating I went back to my corner full of confidence. Perhaps that was my downfall. People always said that all I lacked was self-belief, but that first round gave me too much of it. I opened up, thinking if I put him down twice in the first I could do it again. We exchanged some vicious shots. Boy, was that guy strong.

At the beginning of the third, he caught me flush with a big right that sent me to the canvas. My first pro knockdown. I didn't know what to think but quickly realised I wasn't badly shaken, so got up and went back at him, landing lovely shots to head and body. That guy just kept coming. No matter what I hit him with, I couldn't drive him back.

He was hurt a few times but he would just close the distance and wing hooks. He was so crude and I thought I was doing the better work, the cleaner work, but it was definitely one hell of a scrap. The whole thing turned into a heated 50-50 battle. For the last three rounds it just went back and forth. The commentators on Coldwell TV were going crazy. The crowd were on their feet, screaming. Loads of people told me afterwards it was the best fight they had ever seen. We both gave and took everything.

At the end of six rounds of madness, the referee, Phil Edwards, gave a 58–55 decision to Ambomo. I couldn't believe it. Bainsey, in my corner couldn't believe it. Dave couldn't believe it.

It was tight and you could have argued a round either way. Maybe a draw would have been a fair result, but a three-point margin? What fight had the ref been watching? It didn't help that he hadn't scored my second knockdown.

I felt really deflated – another loss. In the post-fight interview for the TV cameras I tried to put a positive spin on it.

'I'm devastated,' I said, 'but I like to provide entertainment to the crowd and they definitely got that tonight. I used to be a nervous fighter, but not anymore. I come for a fight now!'

The audience around me whooped and roared.

'I'd like a rematch though,' I continued. 'I don't think that was a fair decision.'

Everyone said it was a contest they wanted to see again. Dave was happy. In fact he was more than happy, he was elated.

'You did fantastic!' he told me. 'Absolutely brilliant fighting heart mate. Very proud of you tonight. A loss isn't a loss when the positive reaction is as big as this. Sometimes an early knockdown can fuck your plan up. You just need to learn and move on. You can build on this!'

Afterwards they interviewed Serge in his dressing room.

'Hostile crowds don't scare me,' he said, in broken English. 'I live in hostel. I come to make fight.'

I was in pieces afterwards. I'd bust a knuckle on Serge's big head and my whole body hurt. There were rope burns on my back and I was covered in cuts and bruises. My eyes, ears, ribs, hips and hands were all swollen and tender. I had an ice bath and tried to sleep.

The next morning wasn't much better. My muscles stiffened up so much Michelle had to help me get dressed and undressed. It was two days before I got up off the sofa.

What took my mind off the pain was the public response. It was incredible. People were calling it fight of the year, fight of the decade, all sorts. My social media pages were bombarded with messages. Former light heavyweight world champion Clinton Woods got in touch. He told me I would win titles. My phone buzzed constantly. That's how quickly fortunes can change in boxing. For the first time in years, things were looking up.

Rematch

ONCE all the excitement from the war with Ambomo settled down, my prospects didn't seem quite so amazing. I had made very little money from the contest. I wasn't any clearer whether Dave would be putting me on his shows in the home corner and if he did, it seemed I had been relegated to a situation where I only got paid in tickets.

There had been lots of public calls for a rematch but Dave said nothing about it. He even mentioned that he'd received a short-notice offer for me to box away a couple of weeks after Ambomo, but turned it down because he knew I wouldn't be ready. When he started to put together the line-up for his next show, scheduled for a couple of months after my fight with Serge, he didn't even mention it to me. It seemed I was facing another gap in my career.

I took a while to recuperate and nurse my wounds. The soreness eased up within a week and I went back to the gym, but my injured knuckle stopped me throwing punches. About ten days after the fight I got a call from a business associate of Dave's. He had never phoned me before.

'I've heard on the grapevine that you're not happy the way Dave is managing you,' he said.

'Who told you that?'

'Never mind about that, Jerome,' he continued. 'Listen, keep this conversation to yourself, okay? I've got a close relationship with Dave and I don't want it to be affected.'

I was intrigued. 'Okay'

'How long is your contract?'

'Three years.'

'The reason I asked is that I've been talking to Clifton Mitchell and he's interested in signing some good fighters. Your name's been mentioned. It would be a TV opportunity. We've got a deal with Channel 5.'

That grabbed my interest.

'Look,' I said, 'all I want is to be given enough notice for a fight so that I can have a proper training camp and to be paid correctly. I know I can do something in the sport and if I've got those things it could work.'

'Well I'm sure we can work something out,' he said. 'We saw your last contest and you put up a great performance, really gutsy and you were unlucky not to get a draw at least, but we were horrified. A fighter with your skills shouldn't be matched up with someone like Ambomo at this stage of their career. He's all wrong for you. I know a lot about him. He's an animal. He's got bags of experience from the amateurs. I've watched him in the gym and he's fierce. He's a brutal, brutal fighter. A manager with your best interests at heart wouldn't put a boxer/mover like you in with someone like that unless there's a title on the line. He's put you in a position where you've got everything to lose and nothing to gain. It's not right.'

'I hear what you're saying,' I said. 'But I took that fight because I wanted it. I thought I could win it. I thought I did win it.'

'I appreciate that Jerome. But your manager shouldn't just be offering you whatever fights come along and leaving it up to you. That's not management, that's just being a booking agent. He should be picking opponents for you to advance your career. Right now you need some good testing fights to push you towards titles, not all-out wars like that. Those are the sort of fights that put miles on the clock.'

I thanked him for his advice and he told me he would be back in touch soon to flesh out a deal. I never heard from him again.

Part of the reason for that might be that soon after that unexpected conversation, Dave suddenly pulled his finger out and organised the rematch. Same venue as the last one, same deal with the tickets, six rounds. The show was going to be the first Coldwell event screened on Matchroom Fight Pass and Dave wanted to make sure he had at least one guaranteed crowd pleaser on the bill.

The idea got me excited. The fight was hotly anticipated and Eddie Hearn would be at ringside. You never know, if I gave a great performance in front of Eddie, he might come to me with a fat contract. Stranger things have happened. Dave said as much himself.

'It's a huge opportunity for all our boxers,' he said.

'Great stuff. I'll put on an even better fight than last time.' I replied.

We set the weight limit at 10st 3lb again, a catchweight, and my only stipulation was that Serge needed to be held to it. I had been easy-going the last time and that had probably played into his hands. I wouldn't make the same mistake again.

Locally the build-up generated a massive buzz. Before long it turned nasty. There were people on his side who didn't like that I questioned the decision from the first fight. A lot of nonsense appeared on social media. Serge's girlfriend put all kinds of horrible stuff up. Facebook even removed some of the messages because they were too abusive.

I wasn't sure what was going on, but I got text messages from Serge apologising for what his girlfriend was writing. Comments had been put up under his name, but as his English wasn't very good, I believed he hadn't personally typed them.

'Hi man,' he wrote. 'Just wanted to apologise about the comments Sharon has been making on Facebook. I have tried telling her to stop but she keeps running her mouth off in my name. She has been drinking a lot recently, as a family member has passed away. I hope we can put any differences to one side and just concentrate on the boxing and put on a good show for everyone. We are fighters and professional sportsmen at the end of the day. I have nothing but respect for anyone who enters the ring. Hope your hand is better now and your back to full training. PS. Any banter on Facebook is not down to me. Just wanted to make that clear.'

But then I wondered how he was able to write such long text messages? Was someone else writing those for him too? It was confusing.

I knuckled down with training. There was no question of lacking motivation. I knew how hard this fight would be.

But even with all the hype, as the big night approached it was the same old story with tickets. Two days before I'd sold eight ringside and 38 standard, 46 in total. That gave me £1,890, of which £1,500 was Serge's purse. Dave was surprised.

'Wow,' he said. 'Really thought you would do a few more mate. Shit. Lets just get the weigh-in done and see where we are.'

I told him I hoped to sell at least 20 more before the fight. Again, Dave said he would waive his manager's commission and again, it made me reflect on my mixed feelings.

'I'll only take money off you if you've made more than a grand for yourself,' he said.

I appreciated that. I still felt that Dave was a good guy at heart. He hadn't guided my career in the way he should have but there were times he still treated me well. I think the basic difference was that I viewed boxing as a sport and for me the important thing was what happened in the gym and the ring. Dave and most other people in the game see it as a living and above anything else their priority is pound notes. I could never get my head around that.

I sold a few more at the last minute and my final sales were better than ever before. My misgivings got put behind me. I felt I had something to show the world. I knew I could beat Serge and I wanted to prove it. When I saw him on Sheffield Road, sweating the weight off before the weigh-in, I got straight on to Dave.

'He's overweight again, I'm telling you. We can't have him coming in heavy again.'

Dave got in touch with Serge's trainer, Glyn Rhodes.

'How much is your man weighing?' Dave asked.

'To tell the truth I don't know,' Glyn said. 'I've asked him to get weighed in front of me and he's refused. He's managing that side of it on his own. I don't know what he's up to.'

I wasn't sure if Glyn was trying to play mind games. He's a wily character. I wouldn't put it past him.

On the scales at the Grosvenor, Serge came in at 10st 2¾lb, just inside the weight limit. He looked huge. I wasn't intimidated, but I knew he was up for it. The stare-down was heavy and intense.

'How are you feeling?' Dave asked on the phone, the morning of the fight. 'Ready to take an African to boxing school?'

'I'm feeling confident,' I told him. 'Relaxed and strong. I'm ready to box and if needed, war!'

It was sunny as I arrived at the venue, mid-afternoon with Marvin. The first person I saw in the car-park was Dad.

'Where's your Team Wilson T-shirt?' I asked. I'd had some T-shirts made up for my family to wear.

'I forgot it,' he said.

I got inside, sorted the money out for Serge's wage from my ticket sales and gave it to Spencer Fearn in the office. He nodded his approval, said a few words. I sorted my music, spent a bit of time with Michelle and Serenity, then went back to warm up with Bainsey, throwing hard shots at him, feeling my body heat up and come alive. I loved that feeling, like an engine starting. Then I sat in the chair in the corner, talking to myself.

From there, you know the rest.

Tying Loose Knots

THE doctors were right. Using my memory and brain, writing things down, really did help. Going through the details of my boxing career felt like putting coffee through a filter. There was still bitterness there, but it became palatable.

I still had questions about everything that happened after the first fight with Serge. The idea that we fought a rematch and he knocked me out did not sit well. In my mind was still a different build-up, a different contest, against Rhodes, but up to the first fight, I was pretty clear.

As I had begun using my phone more, I remembered the message from Ambomo and reopened it.

'Hi bro, how are you?'

I replied. It was 12 October, one month on from the fight.

'I'm alive so I'm happy. In pain, but happy. I don't remember our second fight so will need to watch it back when I feel better. I heard what you did at the end which is wrong by the sounds of it. But what's done is done. Well done on winning. Accidents do happen and unfortunately I ended up fighting for my life.'

An hour later, I was resting, picturing a scene of trees cut down in their thousands, dirty ground covered in a swathe of ugly stumps. He responded.

'Cool. Nice to see you're on the mend and pulled through. Yeah accidents do happen, it's boxing. The kiss at the end was just me showing off. I didn't realise you wouldn't get up, but yeah it's all over now. Keep fighting pal.'

I left it there, although I felt unsatisfied. So many knots still needed tying. I knew one day I would have to communicate with Serge again.

It was also becoming more and more obvious that Dad had definitely not died. Not only had he been with me in the hospital on more than occasion since I'd regained consciousness, but as bits of memory came back I remembered seeing him just before the last fight. As it seemed that I hadn't actually fought Ryan, I guessed that meant that the whole dispute with him, Dave and Curtis hadn't happened either. The nasty words, the sports car, Aaron Cornfeld, none of it – that would explain why the three of them were so baffled when I said sorry. I was apologising for things that happened in my old life, one that I lived but they hadn't.

What about Lori? Why hadn't I seen or heard from her since coming out of the coma?

I searched through my text messages and then the contacts list on my phone. There was no Lori Nasri on there. I had no e-mails from her either, or Aaron Cornfeld for that matter. I went on the internet, checked social media sites, put her name into search engines. I couldn't find her. Yet her memory was so vivid, her face, her figure, the texture of her voice, her perfume. Who was she? What was she?

I searched for the pig picture and the message I posted online that started the whole thing. Neither were anywhere to be found. There was a feeling of tightness, almost sickness in my stomach as the realisation grew that none of that stuff seemed to have happened.

On 17 October the hospital therapist came. She said it would be a good idea if I spent some quality time with my family as we'd been apart for a month and a half. She explained that they had a patient's flat at the hospital and we could use it for a while. It would be a good test – they wanted to see how I would cope with being on my own and doing things myself.

I jumped at the idea, so they suggested I go to have a look. I was expecting to find a bare room with a TV and a few beds but I was very pleasantly surprised. The flat had a wide corridor which led to five different rooms. It had a big living room, with three sofas, a 32-inch flatscreen TV mounted on the wall and a landline phone to call outside numbers.

Across from that was a single bedroom, with a smaller TV, an electrical bed and an en-suite bathroom. There was also another double bedroom and a kitchen/ diner, all appliances included. Compared to the ward I had been on it would be like staying in a penthouse suite at the Waldorf Astoria. I could barely believe it. We were granted a stay of two nights and three days. It felt like a holiday.

Michelle arrived with the kids. Everyone was excited and we unpacked everything and settled in. We needed groceries and toiletries, so I suggested a quick trip to the supermarket.

It was one of those things that you say off the cuff without thinking. A visit to the supermarket was a humdrum, mundane event in my old life, but my new reality was different. I put my hard cap on and we headed out.

Leaving the hospital into the evening air made me feel like a mouse between the paws of a huge cat. Unease washed over me as soon as we got in the car. I was actually going out in public. People would see me. Not necessarily sympathetic people either. What if someone got rude or had a go at Michelle and the kids? I wouldn't be able to do a thing.

We pulled up outside the shop and my anxiety increased. I noticed physical symptoms I had only really experienced before when fighting. My heart sped, my breath became short and my limbs hummed with nerves. I suddenly felt doubly aware of the hat and my appearance. I didn't want to get out. The eyes of strangers were everywhere. What would they think? I was no longer like them. I was a freak.

It took a few minutes. I closed my eyes and spoke to myself.

'Face your fear. You *can* overcome this. It's not a big deal.'

Eventually I sucked up some oxygen, stepped on to the concrete and walked tentatively to the entrance. I felt different, estranged, an outsider. I didn't belong there.

It was an ordeal, that shopping trip, but I survived. I kept my eyes down. In the queue one guy looked at my hat and said, 'Did you leave your horse outside?'

I felt like explaining the whole thing to him, but thought better of it. I just smiled and let him enjoy his joke. The tension didn't begin to leave me until we got back in the car.

Maybe I stored up too much anxiety while shopping, but that first night in the family flat was a disaster. We had some dinner and sat down to watch TV, but by 11 I had got tired and went to bed. As I lay there, I began to feel pain in my stomach. It got steadily worse. Within minutes I was nauseous.

I sat on the edge of the bed, retching, burping, passing wind, feeling dizzy and sweating. We weren't sure of the cause but it seemed I had reacted badly to something I had eaten. As my symptoms became worse, Michelle began going through my medication. She checked my anti-seizure tablets and discovered I had missed a dose. We both began to worry that I was going to have another epileptic fit.

Michelle called down for help and within minutes staff came to take me back to my hospital bed. Once there I threw up twice more and stared at the ceiling, unable to sleep. In the morning I returned to the flat and said hello to them all again, exhausted, but pleased they were there.

Over the days that followed, my progress continued and I was informed that I had done well enough to be moved to the rehab centre (Osborn 4, Northern General Hospital). I buzzed with joy, thinking that my troubles were coming to an end. From then on I made of point of doing as many things by myself as possible, so they could see I was independent and didn't need much help. I just wanted to get out of there. It was how I imagine prisoners must feel when their sentence is about to end.

On the day I was scheduled to move I was determined to walk out of the building and not be pushed out. I threw all of my clothes and personal belongings on to the wheelchair seat and walked through the doors and on to the waiting ambulance. It gave me a little feeling of triumph.

Rehab became more intensive at the Northern General. I had daily psychology sessions and visits to the hospital gym. We worked on mobility and stretching exercises for my neck, back, legs and arms. I'd do light, low-intensity 15-to-30-minute cardio sessions on the indoor gym bike. It was amazing how hard I found it, feeling sweaty and out of breath in no time. They observed me walking upstairs and watched me in the kitchen to see if I was able to make hot drinks safely.

On the 28th I got the worst headache I've ever had in my life. It felt like someone was squeezing my temples with an enormous pair of pliers. My head started to swell. They placed me on alert and told me to inform someone immediately if the pain got any worse. Eventually it settled down and they diagnosed high stress.

The following day I was informed that on Friday 31 October, Halloween, seven weeks after the fight and five and a half since I regained consciousness, I would be allowed to check out and go home.

On the Thursday my barber Errol came to sort my hair out for the grand homecoming. It was a strange feeling, having him buzz-cut over the area with no skull. The clippers vibrated against my brain, sending little electrical impulses down my spine. I've known him a long time and trusted him to be careful. We had a good chat about everything. I always enjoy speaking to Errol. He made me feel good.

On the day they gave me printed sheets of exercises I could perform at home. Then at 1pm I was kicked out of my room to make way for another patient. They moved me and all my belongings to the dining room. I had to wait there for hours while they sorted the paper work and medication.

I killed time browsing the internet. After waiting five hours to get a flu jab it turned out it hadn't been ordered correctly. They said I was still discharged, but I'd have to come back the next day to get it done. And that was it. I left. I zoned out of the journey and as I sat in the taxi, a scene played behind my eyes of a mountain crumbling, showering gravel on the scorched ground below. I got home at 5.30pm.

Where The Heart Is

IT was lovely to be allowed home and I spent the night at my Mum's in Sheffield. Being there was both strange and comforting. I stayed a couple of days then headed up to Bradford to see Serenity and my step-kids. Michelle was entering the third trimester of pregnancy and I wanted to be there for her as much as possible.

While I was in hospital she had a scare. One of her scans had failed to detect a heartbeat. Fortunately it turned out the little one was just playing hide and seek behind the placenta, so all was still well. The amount of stress the baby already endured in the womb was a worry. His Mum had been to hell and back. I hoped and prayed he was okay.

I quickly learnt not to push myself too hard. Tiredness came so easily, so I kept things light and exercised only when I had enough energy to do so. It soon became clear that being at home would in some ways present tougher challenges than being in hospital.

Before I always had my release to look forward to, like a goal. Now I saw only a long, slow journey without a clear end point. In hospital there was routine and everything planned for me. Once they let me out, I was left to my own devices.

As the days turned into weeks boredom and frustration set in. I had always been such an active person, so physical. In my old life, most days I would be up from six o'clock and maybe not get home until nine. Most of my waking hours were taken up with work and training. That's the boxing existence.

Now that was gone. The world was just a place outside the window. I watched a lot of TV and found it hard to get to sleep at nights. Sometimes I would still be there, staring at night-time programmes or movies until three or four in the morning.

I felt so unsure and just wanted to be seen as normal, whatever that is. I wanted to do normal things in a normal way. Anything physical was out of the question but I had enjoyed the hospital card games with Marvin. I could still play well. I thought if I went out with him and some friends to a casino, it would help me to convince myself and others that I was all right.

We went to a place in Bradford which was fine because no one knew my face. In Sheffield people might recognise me. Still, people saw me with my cap on and said, 'Are you getting ready for the Grand National?' or things like that. I'd have to explain to them why I was wearing it, which made me self-conscious. They were usually nice and wished me well, but it was still a reminder.

I just had to do it though. I needed to be out and about. I wanted to feel real. It soon became a regular thing, several nights a week, out all night, playing cards.

I played Texas hold 'em for weeks on end. Most times I was standing up from the table with a grand or so. My best win was just over three thousand. That's after going in with £50. Not bad for a guy with brain damage!

Doctors had said I should be resting as much as possible. But it was the one thing I had to connect myself to the old me. It seemed important.

It became a buzz and an adrenaline hit but obviously I couldn't stay in the casino all the time, so I started looking around for other ways to indulge. Before long I was playing roulette on the internet at home. I started playing more and more, winning some, losing some, winning again. It became harder and harder to leave it alone.

About two months after I was discharged from hospital I logged on one evening and paid £500 into the account. I said to myself that if I got up to £3,000, I'd withdraw the winnings and call it a night.

I reached £3,000 almost straight away, like ten minutes or something. I've never had a game like it, I was just flying – win, win, win, win, win, win. So I decided to play on.

Before I knew it I got up to £11,000, kept going, then lost it all. I felt terrible, so I deposited another £500 and started again. I thought if I made it to £11,000 once, I can repeat it. Then I can stop and be happy.

I was back at £11,000 in no time. It was like something from a movie. I felt like I was possessed. The numbers kept going up and up; £15,000, £20,000, £30,000. It was the most amount of money I'd ever had in my grasp in one go. The scar on my head started itching.

I took pictures of what I was doing and sent them to my brother. He called me straight away. 'Jerome,' he said. 'Withdraw the money and put it into your bank account. You could really use that money. Stop playing now.'

I scratched my scar, ignored him and carried on. I got up to £50,000. I didn't even have a smile on my face. Something in my head set that as a new minimum limit. I decided to keep playing, but whatever I did I wouldn't drop below 50 grand. I was staking one and a half, two grand a spin. I've never played like that before in my life. Never.

I had an idea to try to make it to £100,000, but it was more than an idea. Somehow I just knew I could do it. The skin around my injury itched and itched, while every spin, my numbers kept coming up. Every time. I knew what they would be before I pressed the key. It was as if I was controlling the game.

Seventy, 80, 90 grand. I just kept going and going. Some of the individual spins I won as much as £15,000. By four in the morning I'd hit £102,000. I took a picture and sent it to Marvin. He called me again, straight away, 'Stop playing now! Are you mad? That could change your life!'

While we were on the phone I missed a couple of spins and I saw that the numbers that came up were the ones I had been playing. I was furious! He'd distracted me. I could have gone up to £130,000! So I put the phone down and decided to carry on. My head stopped itching.

For some reason I wasn't reading the numbers like before. Because the winnings were so high, the stakes had gone up and each spin was costing me loads. In one go I was back down to £85,000, then £70,000, then £60,000.

I told myself, if I've done it from £500 I can get back up again. But it was just going down and down.

I'd never experienced that kind of loss of control before. The injury had opened something up, or maybe closed something. My usual limitations weren't there. It felt like great heights and terrible lows were easily reachable, like going up or down a stepladder. The boundaries had been removed. I hadn't even found it exciting.

'I must be crazy,' I thought as I sunk even lower. That's something that people say but don't mean. I meant it. To gamble so recklessly in the way that I did? That's not me. I blew it all by the end, every penny.

I'd been up all night. I was so annoyed with myself. I could have put a deposit down on a house, or secured my future for the next few years with that.

That's when I began to recognise that this thing had changed me in ways I don't understand. No one does, not even the doctors. Since that night I haven't gambled again. I didn't have any control. I scared myself.

I was like a puppet. I have no idea who was controlling the strings.

I lied to Michelle and told her that I collected £10,000, because I didn't want her to think I was a fool. When the truth came out she was really annoyed. I can't blame her, either.

Without the gambling I was back to having nothing to do. I felt so useless and lifeless and my twisted moods darkened. I began to think about suicide.

'I must be such a disappointment to them all,' I thought.

I began boxing as a teenager aiming for glory, but there's no glory in sitting indoors all day with a quarter of your head missing. I was doing so very little to contribute to the family. Maybe they'd be better off without me? It would be easy, I thought. I'm on so much medication anyway. One night, when the house is quiet, I could just take the lot, knock the pills back with a shot of rum. I don't drink much, but it seemed a fitting way to end it. I would be free. They would all benefit financially. They could claim on the life insurance. At least I could provide them that.

I battled those feelings in a private war. I made lists of reasons not to do it. Life is a gift. Many would miss me. I was stupid to think like that. Things would get better.

Before long Christmas approached and I tried to be positive for the kids. Money was tight, but we took Serenity to the cinema to see *Paddington Bear*. Still I sometimes found myself dwelling on what might have been.

As the film played out I drifted away from the story and thought how I would never get to feel what it is like to hold a belt. To be proud of my achievements like Curtis or Ryan or Kell. I couldn't help but feel that boxing had screwed me over and treated me like a mug. By the time the film finished I resolved that all I'd done in the past was get through everything as best as I could. And that's all I could keep doing from then on.

Early in the New Year I was watching *Ringside* on Sky Sports. As they discussed the week's boxing news, I was overcome with sadness again. I was missing training and fighting so much. It must have shown on my face.

Serenity was next to me on the sofa. She looked up and said, 'What's wrong daddy?'

'Nothing baby, I'm okay.' I replied.

'I can I get you your tablets if you want.'

I had to laugh.

The Value Of Sanity

NO matter how positive I tried to be as I looked to the future, one problem was difficult to get past. Before my injury my income had come from personal training, supplemented by boxing. I was now unable to do either of those things. My boxing friends had worked really hard to raise money for me and the British Boxing Board of Control had paid out £2,000 from its charity fund. It was nice to receive and much appreciated but it wouldn't keep me going for more than a couple of months.

My inability to work spread beyond the short-term, too. Sure I was lucky compared to some. Guys with my sort of injury either never recovered or spent years disabled. I was suffering memory and psychological issues, but at least I was walking and talking. Yet the craniectomy meant even leaving the house was an ordeal and something as simple as writing an e-mail or having a conversation left me exhausted.

I am stuck with these symptoms for the foreseeable future, at least until I had my next operation, to have a metal plate bolted into my head. That wasn't scheduled until August 2015. There were no guarantees how well I would recover after that either. The neurological difficulties I was facing, caused by my time in the ring, could stay with me forever. Other boxers like Spencer Oliver and Audley Harrison offered advice, but there was always the chance that I could deteriorate, suffer from pugilistica dementia and need full-time care in later life.

Boxing may be a business, but it had to have some sporting ethics involved somewhere, surely? I found the board had an insurance policy. It had been set up after the Watson situation, when he was knocked out by Chris Eubank at White Hart Lane in 1991. The doctors had said that my injury was almost exactly the same. The only difference was that Michael's recovery was much slower.

In February, six months after the second Ambomo fight, I wrote to the board to ask if I could claim, suggesting that at some point I might consider coaching and so any money I was offered could contribute to the sport in future. I received a reply from Robert Smith, the general secretary. His reply was not very encouraging.

Dear Jerome,
RE:- GYM DONATION

Thank you for your e-mail, I am pleased you are looking to stay in the sport and hopefully you will be applying to the Central Area Council for a Trainer/ second licence, which will enable you to train boxers at your gym.

With regard to compensation, the Board do not pay out compensation for injuries but have an insurance policy which covers loss of life and permanent injury. My understanding is that you have made a good recovery and therefore are not entitled to an insurance pay-out.

The Board's Charity has already paid out a donation to you following your injury and should you require financial assistance to set up your gym, I am sure the Board Stewards will consider a further donation to purchase some gym equipment.

When you are in a position to do so, supply a list of equipment required and I can talk to the members of the Board on your behalf.

Once again, thank you for your e-mail and good luck.

Yours sincerely,
Robert Smith

I wrote back, explaining that to that point I had not been able to work and that it was unclear when or if I ever would be. Indeed that all medical evidence was that I would never return to full health. I had a quarter of my skull missing and complicated psychological symptoms.

His response was brief.

Dear Jerome,
Thank you for your e-mail, all reports received have been positive regarding your recovery, which is extremely good news.

Should you decide to apply for a Trainer/second licence in the future, please do so by requesting the appropriate form from Head Office.

Good luck in your new venture.

Yours Sincerely,

Robert Smith

Initially I was shocked. It seemed that having paid me the equivalent of a month's average salary from its charity fund, the board had no intention of assisting me with my continued recovery or looking after my family. As far as I was aware it had sought no medical advice, spoken to no doctors or used any of form of evidence at all to support its belief that I had recovered well.

Psychological damage is a stigmatised and misunderstood thing. I was no longer the Jerome Wilson I once had been. My head was full of memories that never happened, I was depressed and experiencing loss of control. I had self-destructive urges and thoughts, but for the purposes of insurance none of that mattered. I wasn't blind, I wasn't deaf and I could walk by myself, so I had made 'a good recovery'. The only way I would be able to pursue the matter further would be legally.

The solicitor I found confirmed that under the terms of the policy I was not eligible to claim, but was staggered that the governing body of such a dangerous professional sport could operate with these stipulations. He believed that the whole system needed to be changed so that this was explained to every fighter at the outset, with provisions set out in law.

Wiped Out? The Jerome Wilson Story

How can the board just allow injured boxers to be thrown on the scrapheap? What am I expected to do now? Claim disability and sit in the house?

Welcome To Cairo

I TRIED to use the first few months of 2015 to get myself back into some sort of gear. My sleep patterns were still all over the place and my anxiety and mood swings continued, but I did a few radio and TV interviews. The opportunity to start work on this book came up too. It's been helpful to channel my thoughts into something and get it all down on paper. It's given me something to work towards.

In January we went for Michelle's four-month scan. For the first time we saw our baby's features. They told us we were having a boy.

We saw him moving about and heard his heart beat. He had plenty of fluid around him. They said he was a good size. His heart was functioning well.

The fact that this little one had even survived so far was amazing to me. He must be a real fighter! For that reason this baby is very, very special. He represents my hopes for better things, being be born out of the worst possible time – a positive to come from all the bad.

On 18 February at 3.30am, all of that was suddenly thrown into doubt. Michelle woke up in bed alone. I had stayed up late watching TV and fallen asleep on the sofa. She was in terrible pain.

She managed to bring herself down to the kitchen and put the kettle on. In the end that's what woke me up, the sounds of the kettle and voices. Michelle and Calvin were talking anxiously.

I got up groggily and asked what was wrong. She was distressed. Her eyes were full of tears.

'I have a ripping pain on the right side of my belly,' she said. There was panic in her voice. 'It's agony.'

That didn't sound good. I tried to reassure her. We called the hospital. They asked some questions then told her to come straight in.

Calvin called a taxi and as we waited, we rushed around grabbing things from the house. Baby notes, a hospital bag, her baby bag, her jacket and hat. The driver set off like he was on a milk float. It was a tortuous journey, so slow, with Michelle wincing and crying. Fifteen minutes later we arrived at hospital.

Michelle had to give a urine sample so I accompanied her to the toilet. We then needed to check that the baby's vital signs. The nurse hooked her up to the heart monitor and performed other tests, then assured us the baby was fine.

They came to the conclusion that Michelle was in the early stages of labour, but she was only seven months pregnant. They decided to try to stop it by giving a steroid injection in her buttock to strengthen the baby's lungs and tablets to delay labour.

From there, everything became a blur.

Minutes after swallowing the second tablet Michelle begun to feel hot and started to sweat. I pressed the buzzer. Doctors and nurses came flying in and put Michelle on a drip in to give her some fluids, in the hope of raising her blood pressure. The baby's heart rate plummeted.

Unfortunately the drip had no effect and things continued to get worse. The room was hectic. I couldn't help but think back to my own time in hospital just a few months previously. It seemed like a re-run, but with the roles reversed. I held Michelle's hand and tried to reassure her that all would be okay. Inside I panicked.

Michelle kept repeating that she felt sick. The colour drained from her face and she looked like she was losing consciousness. They were grim moments.

'Don't worry,' I kept saying, squeezing her hand. 'They know what they're doing,' hoping desperately that the medical staff would sort it all out. The world stood still for a while. Things were happening around us and we were just in a bubble in the middle.

The anaesthetist came in and started asking Michelle all sorts of questions. No one had told us anything yet. I knew at that point something was seriously wrong.

Someone pulled me to one side and explained that the situation had become an emergency. The baby would have to be delivered straight away. His heart rate was still falling and Michelle's blood pressure was dangerously low.

They wheeled her out of the room as fast as possible. Everyone was shouting. The wheels of the bed rattled on the floor as they took her into theatre for an emergency cesarean section. I waited outside. When I closed my eyes I saw a lake of green water, with puffy, bloated fish bobbing on the surface. I felt numb.

As time dragged on my worry turned to fear. If it had been simple it would surely have happened quickly. An hour later a nurse came into the room and sat down beside me.

She spoke quietly.

'Your son has been delivered,' she said. 'But he's in a bit of distress, and needs help breathing. You can go and see him in a minute before he has to be moved to the baby special care unit.'

'And Michelle?' I asked.

'She's very poorly at the moment, but the operation went well.'

They had discovered that Michelle's symptoms had been due to the placenta coming away, and internal bleeding. The nurse assured me that Michelle should be fine in the end but would need a while to recover. I broke down in tears. It was overwhelming. I had never been so frightened in my life.

The official time of the birth was 6.47am. I had been up all night, in hospital with my hard-hat on, but the little man had made it. Welcome to the world Cairo Jerome Jr. Wilson. He was the tiniest baby I had ever seen. If I could have picked him up he would have fit into the palm of my hand.

Michelle recovered well and four days later, on the 22nd, we were given the all clear to leave hospital. She was back into routine in no time, such a strong woman.

In the twilight of morning, on the 24th, I was woken up by Serenity. There was urgency in her voice.

'Get up Daddy, get up!'

I woke in a panic. What's happened now? There's only so much drama a family can take.

Michelle stood behind her. I looked from one to the other. Together they shouted, 'Happy birthday!'

I laughed out loud – I had clean forgotten, it had been such a crazy period of my life. Thirty years old. That's where life begins isn't it?

Cairo still slept and Michelle got the rest of the kids ready. They all went off on the school run and I was left in a quiet house with my tiny son. I sat over his crib, staring at him. Before long he began to stir, ready for his next feed. I got it ready, talking to him.

'Daddy's going to sort it out for you. Just lie still.' Before long he was in my arms, sucking on the bottle.

At that moment things felt different. For the first time in my new life and maybe my old one too, I had a feeling of peace. It would be an unusual birthday, my 30th. No partying and messing around, but you know what? That's okay. Maybe that's some kind of wisdom, right there.

As Cairo finished his milk I said, 'Thank you.'

I don't know who I was talking to.

Looking For Serge

BACK in the hospital, when Marvin told me what Ambomo did at the end of our second fight, I had been disgusted. Marvin called him 'an excuse for a human being'. I tended to agree.

There had been a suggestion of him coming to visit me on the ward but I didn't want anything to do with that. It was too soon. Before I thought about communicating with him I would need to sort out my own feelings. I remembered how brutal our first fight had been. I remembered all the credit I got from boxing people for that. Dave, guys in the gym, fans who had seen it, they all said how I had proved myself, a true warrior. The words I always wanted to hear.

The rematch probably wasn't right for me. Many said they were surprised it happened. Dave had just signed his Fight Pass deal with Eddie Hearn and wanted to impress him. It may be that was more important than protecting my interests. But Dave can't take all the blame. I wanted the rematch. Wanted it badly. I kept asking for it.

Should Dave have advised me against it? That's pure opinion. I know boxing is a business. I've had that repeatedly drilled into my ears since I started. I don't like it, but I know it. I also know that Dave is a businessman. But from the beginning I believed he was also my friend.

Sometimes I do look back at those two fights and wonder. All the away corner offers that kept coming up against O'Maison and Witter and the rest. Was I being set up to lose? To be turned into a human punchbag? I won't ever know the answer to that.

As the change from old to new life has cemented, the hardest thing to accept is that it was really a second fight with Serge that left me like this. I've watched the film of it now, so I know it's true.

The second bout wasn't quite as mad as the first one, as far I can see. I boxed well in round one, boxed to my strengths, but from round two he closed the distance and turned it into a war. He knocked me down, I got up. I was giving the crowd what they wanted, what Dave always said he wanted. It was take two, land two, him and me, then right at the death, he got me. When Ambomo kissed my head, then made the throat-cutting sign, I thought of Russell Crowe in *Gladiator*, shouting, 'Are you not entertained?' over his opponent's carcass. Isn't that what they really want to see, on some level what it's all about?

At the back of my mind was always the idea that I would get in touch with Serge once I watched the video. The recording had never been made publicly available on the internet, for obvious reasons, but the guys from Matchroom Fight Pass sent me a closed link.

In March I messaged him. It was the first contact we had for five months.

'I always said that I would tell you what I thought of the fight after I watched it back in full. Watched it for the first time on Saturday. You won the fight, but what you did after was very disrespectful, regardless if you knew what state I was in or not. What's done is done, just telling you what I thought.'

Serge replied.

'I'm glad you're on the mend. Yeah I won the fight and I always apologised for the showboating and I had to take it on the chin. The hate mail I was getting wasn't fair at all, if it would have been the other way around it would be a different story. Anyway I'm glad you're okay and good luck in what you do.'

A few more words were exchanged. It got quite heated. There's still bad feeling there.

I've spoken to many people about it since. Glyn Rhodes managed and trained him, but isn't having much to do with Serge anymore. One or two others said the suspension from boxing hit him hard and he went off the rails a bit.

More than anything else, when I think about it, I'm just upset that I lost. I know I can beat Serge Ambomo, no matter what it says on our records. There's a part of me that wants nothing more than to fight him again, but I know that can never happen.

My trainer Bainsey summed it up. 'You were easily the better boxer Jerome.' He said. 'But Ambomo was more of a fighter.'

Perhaps I didn't have enough brawling instinct, or perhaps I was foolish to brawl with a brawler. There's no point over-analysing it now. I do think that soon I will be ready to forgive him. In fact, I know I must. After my next operation I plan to arrange a meeting, with a friend of mine who can translate, as he speaks French.

My new life can't flourish if it's planted in resentment, I believe that. Growth begins from the root. Sometimes I think, 'If I wasn't in that fight, I wouldn't be like this. If Witter or O'Maison had fulfilled their commitments... If Dave... What if this? What if that?'

You can go on forever.

I'm going to try different things, reading, learning, setting challenges. In the future I have grand targets. Run marathons, climb mountains, become my own master. One day, I will get there.

Reconnection

BY summer 2015 I had understood that the mental aspects of my injury are far worse than the physical ones. I've felt down and been in dark places in my mind, but hid it from people around me. I refuse to let them see me so weak and in need of help. Come on! I'm a fighter.

I mean, I was.

People have always viewed me as strong and positive, as a person who helps others, but even though the doctors drained the blood on the night, I have so much pressure in my head. The headaches still come. Sometimes I drift for days. I'd never like to describe myself as depressed but I don't know what else to call it. I do feel lost.

In April I called the outpatients department at the hospital and asked if I could speak to a psychiatrist. It was the first time I had sought that kind of help. They said they would put that in place after my next operation. I'm still waiting. Hopefully soon it will be done.

Reconnection

I know I'm strong enough to deal with this. I am a tough guy, remember – a fighter.

I mean, I was.

I must be grateful for the support I've had. My family, my friends and my old colleagues from the boxing world have been amazing. I often feel I don't deserve it. The future can still be a good one for my family and me. I do believe that. You can grow from every experience, no matter what. I wish sometimes I could talk to my younger self, or lend him my eyes.

I see so much further now than dreams and glory. My vision is filled with the space dug out of my skull. That pride, that furious desire to prove myself and show my worth, I will one day carry that back to the earth with me.

Boxing couldn't satisfy it and injury didn't remove it. It lives on. And so do I.

For now I'm waiting on the date of my next operation, a craniotomy to put a titanium plate in the hole in my head. It's a risky procedure. They gave me an option not to go through with it, but it's something I want. Without it, there's no chance of a normal life again.

I've been prescribed anti-depressants for the feelings I've had. They're sitting in a jar on a high shelf in the kitchen. I haven't touched them yet. I'm scared if I do I might become dependent. I suppose they're there if one day I really cannot cope.

I already have to take tablets for my mad headaches. Sometimes it feels like my brain's so swollen it will pop out of my head and on to the floor. I have spine and chest pain too.

I'm on epilepsy prevention pills, to decrease the chances of another seizure. I've been on them since the fight. If I have another fit now it would probably finish me off. Even sneezing is strange, frightening and painful.

Every night when I go to bed, the area around the injury swells. My brain-tissue becomes turgid, rises like bread in the oven and presses against the skin. In the morning I can put my finger against the scar and touch my own brain. It feels boggy, like a waterbed. What a crazy sensation.

I want to smile and be brave – everyone loves a battler! But I do struggle to find motivation. Sometimes I can't summon the energy to do simple things like brush my teeth at night. That would never happen before my injury.

I stay in bed a lot. When I do get up my legs are weak. I keep forgetting things, especially people's names. Sometimes even people I know quite well. Some days it's a real effort to speak.

Decisions have become such a challenge. Shall I have something to eat? Shall I watch a film? Yes, no, yes, no. I can go back and forwards for hours before I do anything. I guess I'm a bit directionless.

I can't cook alone. I can't drive my car. I have to be extra careful when I play with my kids. Any little knock could mean trouble, so I have to be chaperoned when I leave the house. What if something falls on my head? I'm always looking up, warily.

One of the worst things is the mirror. They used to say if you look in the mirror for too long you see the devil in there. Sometimes I think that's true.

But I'll be okay. I'm a fighter, remember.

I mean, I was.

How have I changed? It's hard to say, in all ways. It feels like my brain has knit back together, but differently. New life has brought new perspective.

One day in March, I put my hard hat on and walked up to Serenity's nursery to collect her, alone. It was the first time. Michelle had been doing everything, as well as looking after me.

It was making her so tired. I wanted to help. I had some sweets with me, as a treat for Serenity being good.

She laughed and jumped when she saw me, then came running over. I guess it was fun and unusual to be picked up by Daddy. I felt all right being out on my own, so decided to take her to the local park, just the two of us. We could have some time together.

The playground was empty when we arrived.

'Push me on the swings, Daddy?' Serenity asked.

'Okay! Do you want me to push you high in the sky?'

'Yes, yes!'

I looked up. It was quite a cold day, but bright and clear. I lifted her up into the seat and began to push. I felt an enormous surge of love, a great connection, within me and beyond. It was overpowering. The sun, the air, the giant smile on her face, they were all part of the same thing.

'Push higher, Daddy! Higher!

To begin with I laughed with her, nudging the back of the swing, her little legs dangling, watching her disappear up into the sun. I laughed with her. I laughed like her, like I hadn't laughed for months. I laughed like a child.

Then almost without noticing, my chest heaved and I started to cry. Laughter turned to tears, great pearls of water. They rolled down my face and dripped down, swallowed by the ground. I thought of my next operation, wondering if I would make it out alive. I thought of the possibility that I would lose my mind by middle age, become unaware, that there would be no more moments of beauty. How would Michelle cope? How would little Serenity manage without me?

I put my hands on her shoulders, felt her live below my fingers. Like a hook to the jaw, it struck me. Our energy is shared. I will always be Jerome and so will she.

The operation looms large in my future, like a stay of execution. I've never been a weak man, never a frightened one, not publicly anyway. As the date approaches, it's like looking forward to a fight. Well, almost, but not quite. There's one major difference. Before a fight I refused to feel fear. I refused to acknowledge it.

When I imagine the op, they are such charged moments, so emotional. I fear losing everything. I fear not fighting. I get butterflies, nervous tension and fear. I have to call call it fear. Definitely fear.

Am I a fighter? I know I was.

The most common complication is that a blood clot can develop at the site of the surgery. This would mean another emergency procedure. If that happens I could be back to square one.

Reconnection

I have been told of the possibility of nerve damage, causing muscle weakness or even paralysis, stroke, memory loss, impaired mental or cognitive functions and, of course, a small chance of death.

When I go back to hospital and they put me under anaesthetic, I sometimes wonder if I will go back to my old life. I still expect to bump into Lori Nasri one day. She remains important to me.

I don't believe that she's not 'real', whatever that means. I carried on searching, with no joy. I've managed to accept that she doesn't and never did exist in this world. Not in this time.

I often ask why that version of things shouldn't be true. Maybe she did come into my life, maybe my Dad was killed. Maybe I did fight Ryan.

They say you can't dream while comatose. So what if it wasn't a dream? What if this is?

This could all be part of it. Hospital, going home, watching the tape of fighting Serge, gambling, Cairo's birth, the family issues, this book – it feels exactly the same.

Common sense says that my old life was imaginary – some kind of coma nightmare, but it also tells me it was far too detailed for that. I believe I was transported to an alternative reality, maybe some kind of other dimension, where I lived a different life, where I was a different Jerome.

Maybe we all have many different lives happening at once. Right now I have been chosen for this one, but for a while I got to live another. These are the things I think about now.

Truth is only what you perceive.

Humans

I remember as a kid someone saying your whole life is a dream and when you die, you wake up.

Who knows? You can drive yourself crazy thinking about it. Too much of that and you end up on the happy pills.

I am Jerome Wilson, ex-fighter.

And I'm lucky to be alive.

Epilogue From The Author

SERGE Ambomo was given the opportunity to express his side of the story in this book but declined to do so.

After knocking Jerome out, at the end of the second fight, he crouched over him and kissed his head.

Facing vicious abuse from supporters around the ring, he then stood by the ropes and made a throat-cutting gesture at the audience with one hand. He cannot have known how critical Jerome's condition was, but even for boxing crowds who routinely thrill at violence and are excited by blood, he had crossed a line of acceptability.

Dave Coldwell jumped up into the ring to remonstrate with him. After putting Jerome into the recovery position, Glyn Rhodes pushed Serge back to the corner, slapped his face and gave him a telling off. He may have won but the man from Cameroon had no real opportunity to celebrate.

In the aftermath the British Boxing Board of Control suspended his licence. Months later he was summoned to a hearing to explain his actions but failed to attend. He was in custody, having been arrested the night before for street-brawling in Rotherham.

The board gave Serge a £3,000 fine. As an asylum seeker, staying in temporary accommodation and surviving day to day, it was an impossible sum to pay. He could not box until it was settled but his only income came from boxing.

A lifeline was thrown by another promoter who saw in him the potential for titles. He offered to buy out his contract and pay the fine to get him fighting again. However Serge still owed money to his current manager and the sponsors that had been arranged for him upon turning pro. Until these debts were covered, he would be stuck in limbo. His future as a fighter appeared doubtful.

For his part Ambomo has publicly apologised. He professes to be a Christian and texted Jerome saying that he prayed for him every night. Glyn Rhodes is convinced that his regret is sincere. He also states that Serge was genuinely upset at not being able to visit Jerome in hospital.

There is no way around the fact that what Ambomo did was regrettable and disrespectful, yet it must be placed in the context of a heated build-up, a hostile arena and the climax of two adrenaline-filled, utterly chaotic boxing matches. Perhaps he has paid his price now. The individual reader can decide on that. He should not be thought of as some kind of pantomime villain.

Epilogue From The Author

What is indisputable is that these two intense bouts exemplified everything that fight fans find so thrilling and outsiders find so horrifying. They profoundly affected both young men involved. Yes, crowds were entertained. Yes, internet viewing figures were bolstered. Yes, the stock of managers and promoters rose, but in many ways both fighters lost.

One ended up with a quarter of his skull missing and his life hanging by a thread. His livelihood gone, he now fights only for his sanity. The other faces poverty, unable to practice the only profession he knows. As this book went to press, a year on from that ill-fated night, he still had not fought again.

Surrounding the upper echelons of the professional ring, where champions and millions are made, there is a world of concoction and myth, of stories grown larger through retelling. That has not been needed here. No titles were contested in the two Wilson v Ambomo fights. They were six round, undercard matches, yet no one who saw them will ever forget their drama – their pitiless, provocative, life-altering drama.

This is boxing.

Further Acknowledgements

J EROME Wilson would like to thank the following people who assisted in his career or recovery:

All Team Wilson sponsors: Ace Janitorials, CLL Solicitors, Readhunt Insurance, Motus Exec and Lafarge Tarmac who helped him to pay his medical and boxing license fees for the last year as a pro.

Glyn Rhodes, Dr Hassan, Mark Williams, Ian Baines, Ryan Rhodes, Marvin Wilson, Emma Digby, Mike Huntington, Claire Huntington, Calvin Boyce, Lisa Walton, Michelle Boyce, Stacey Lee, Ryan Lee Scott, Sarah Jayne Toothill, Carly Crosdale, Darren and Allison Busfield, Janet Scott, Jo Allen and Mark Walton, Curtis Woodhouse, Cam Linley and Ash Davison who all helped after the accident.

Thanks also to everyone at Coldwell Boxing team, especially Spencer Fearn, Damian Harry and David Coldwell. And to the guys at Prime Mover Gym: Annaliese Reynolds and Scott Reynolds and all the Prime Mover tribe. Also to everyone at Paleo Fitness:

Further Acknowledgements

Ian Baines, Jamie Kennedy, Mark Brine, Fritz Marsden and all the people who helped to support him.

Alastair Hayes, the local area chairman of the British Boxing Board of Control who came to visit him in hospital and offer support.

All Team Wilson supporters – every single person who purchased a ticket is deeply appreciated. Without them he wouldn't have been able to fight at all. Your support really meant a lot to Jerome. It still does. It always will.

The incredible surgeons, doctors, nurses and therapists at the Sheffield Royal Hallamshire and Northern General hospitals. Without them, he would not be here.

Jerome would like to say to everyone who helped in his time of need, thank you all from the bottom of his heart.

Your prayers helped to give him the strength to get through the most difficult of times.

Nelson Vasconcelos did a great job with the graphic design and video work for this book's promotional materials.

Lastly sincere thanks to Sheffield Newspapers, Mark Crawshaw, Mark J Jones and Neil Webster photography, who provided images free of charge.